Student Workbook

for Verderbers'

Communicate!

Tenth Edition

Student Workbook

for Verderbers'

Communicate!

Tenth Edition

Leonard E. Assante
Volunteer State Community College

WADSWORTH
™

THOMSON LEARNING

Australia • Canada • Mexico • Singapore • Spain • United Kingdom • United States

Assistant Editor: Nicole George
Executive Editor: Deirdre Cavanaugh
Print/Media Buyer: Christopher Burnham

Ancillaries Coordinator: Carrie Fahey
Cover Designer: Jeanne Calabrese Design
Cover Illustrator: Otto Steininger

Printed in Canada
1 2 3 4 5 6 7 05 04 03 02 01

ISBN 0-534-56123-3

For more information, contact
Wadsworth/Thomson Learning
10 Davis Drive
Belmont, CA 94002-3098
USA

For more information about our products, contact us:
Thomson Learning Academic Resource Center
1-800-423-0563
http://www.wadsworth.com

International Headquarters
Thomson Learning
International Division
290 Harbor Drive, 2nd Floor
Stamford, CT 06902-7477
USA

UK/Europe/Middle East/South Africa
Thomson Learning
Berkshire House
168-173 High Holborn
London WC1V 7AA
United Kingdom

Asia
Thomson Learning
60 Albert Complex, #15-01
Singapore 189969

Canada
Nelson Thomson Learning
1120 Birchmount Road
Toronto, Ontario M1K 5G4
Canada

TABLE OF CONTENTS

Acknowledgments

Preface

PART I: FOUNDATION OF COMMUNICATION

Key Terms
Exercises
      Observe and analyze journal
      InfoTrac
      Web-based
Chapter Quiz Questions
Useful and Interesting Internet Links

PART II: INTRODUCTION TO INTERPERSONAL COMMUNIATION

Learning Objectives
Interactive Chapter Outline
Key Terms
Exercises
      Observe and analyze journal
      InfoTrac
      Web-based
Chapter Quiz Questions
Useful and Interesting Internet Links

Learning Objectives
Interactive Chapter Outline
Key Terms
Exercises
      Observe and analyze journal
      InfoTrac
      Web-based
Chapter Quiz Questions
Useful and Interesting Internet Links

Learning Objectives
Interactive Chapter Outline
Key Terms
Exercises
      Observe and analyze journal
      InfoTrac
      Web-based
Chapter Quiz Questions
Useful and Interesting Internet Links

Learning Objectives
Interactive Chapter Outline

Key Terms
Exercises
> Observe and analyze journal
> InfoTrac
> Web-based
Chapter Quiz Questions
Useful and Interesting Internet Links

Learning Objectives
Interactive Chapter Outline
Key Terms
Exercises
> Observe and analyze journal
> InfoTrac
> Web-based
Chapter Quiz Questions
Useful and Interesting Internet Links

Learning Objectives
Interactive Chapter Outline
Key Terms
Exercises
> Observe and analyze journal
> InfoTrac
> Web-based
Chapter Quiz Questions
Useful and Interesting Internet Links

PART III: GROUP COMMUNICATION

Learning Objectives
Interactive Chapter Outline
Key Terms
Exercises
> Observe and analyze journal
> InfoTrac
> Web-based
Chapter Quiz Questions
Useful and Interesting Internet Links

Learning Objectives
Interactive Chapter Outline
Key Terms
Exercises
       Observe and analyze journal
       InfoTrac
       Web-based
Chapter Quiz Questions
Useful and Interesting Internet Links

PART IV: PUBLIC SPEAKING

Learning Objectives
Interactive Chapter Outline
Key Terms
Exercises
       Observe and analyze journal
       InfoTrac
       Web-based
Chapter Quiz Questions
Useful and Interesting Internet Links

Learning Objectives
Interactive Chapter Outline
Key Terms
Exercises
       Observe and analyze journal
       InfoTrac
       Web-based
Chapter Quiz Questions
Useful and Interesting Internet Links

Learning Objectives
Interactive Chapter Outline
Key Terms
Exercises
       Observe and analyze journal
       InfoTrac
       Web-based
Chapter Quiz Questions
Useful and Interesting Internet Links
Outline and Organization Forms

CHAPTER 15: Adapting Verbally and Visually. 244
Learning Objectives
Interactive Chapter Outline
Key Terms
Exercises
       Observe and analyze journal
       InfoTrac
       Web-based
Chapter Quiz Questions
Useful and Interesting Internet Links

CHPATER 16: Practicing the Presentation of Your Speech. 261
Learning Objectives
Interactive Chapter Outline
Key Terms
Exercises
       Observe and analyze journal
       InfoTrac
       Web-based
Chapter Quiz Questions
Useful and Interesting Internet Links

CHAPTER 17: Informative Speaking. 280
Learning Objectives
Interactive Chapter Outline
Key Terms
Exercises
       Observe and analyze journal
       InfoTrac
       Web-based
Organization and Outlining Forms for Informative Speeches
Chapter Quiz Questions
Useful and Interesting Internet Links

CHAPTER 18: Persuasive Speaking. 293
Learning Objectives
Interactive Chapter Outline
Key Terms
Exercises
       Observe and analyze journal
       InfoTrac
       Web-based
Organization and Outlining Forms for Persuasive Speeches
Chapter Quiz Questions
Useful and Interesting Internet Links

Outline and Organization Forms

Speech Interactive for Communicate! on your Communicate! CD-ROM

ACKNOWLEDGEMENTS

I strongly believe that no significant endeavor in life is completed alone or without the influence of others. This text is no exception. Many individuals assisted me in my first major writing project. I would like to especially thank:

-Deirdre Cavanaugh
> For her support, encouragement and interest. Without her I would not be in print today.

-Nicole George
> For her good humor and help in answering countless questions both small and large.

-David Warner
> For his multiple good ideas, encouragement and creativity. For designing a method to keep me on track and motivated.

-Ben Jobe
> For the "Blockbuster approach to teaching speech."

-Stuart Schrader
> For 13 years of encouragement, motivation and friendship.

-The faculty of the Department of Communication at Volunteer State
> For bearing with a first-year Chair and a first-time author

-And, finally, to *Cindy McLeod*, who has love enough to brighten my life, wit enough to make me laugh, intelligence enough to dazzle me, mischief enough to keep me guessing, and sense enough to know a good thing when she sees it. This is for you.

-Leonard Assante, Gallatin, TN

PREFACE

Welcome to the Student Workbook for *Communicate!* by Rudolph and Kathleen Verderber! Congratulations on your decision to enroll in an introductory communication course. Effective communication skills are an important component to a successful career and satisfying interpersonal relationships. When I was asked by my Editor to write the student workbook for *Communicate!*, I was a little uneasy. I knew what a workbook was; I knew it had to contain certain information and resources to go along with the textbook and I knew it had to help students understand and use the concepts the text explores. I knew all the usual stuff about workbooks. But as a teacher who has used texts with workbooks, I also knew that for it to be a truly useful addition to the text (they call it an "ancillary" in the book business), students had to actually *use* it. And use it *regularly*. And use it *often*. The publishers also sent me a bunch of copies of other student workbooks that had been written for other texts. In each of these, I found useful and interesting ideas. What I decided I would try to do was create a book that was hopefully more than a traditional workbook, but actually a companion to the textbook that incorporates both my own ideas and the best of what I have found in reviewing other similar texts. My hope is that you will find this approach useful in your study of communication. This workbook is designed to be used with the textbook in studying for exams, learning key concepts, doing application exercises, researching speeches and taking notes in class. I encourage you to take this book to class along with your textbook, use it to help you take notes, to tie the individual concepts together into the "big picture," and to assist your communication education. Below I list the key objectives of the textbook and course. I then introduce you to the key parts of this book and how they are designed to help you. Good luck!

Textbook Objectives. The textbook is designed to meet several objectives;
- To make the communication process understood by defining and clarifying key terms used to talk about communication.
- To apply communication concepts to situations we encounter in our everyday lives.
- To present guidelines for communication competency and skill development.

Course Objectives. While all communication courses (and communication instructors!) are different, it is very likely that any course that uses *Communicate!* has the following objectives:
- Define and describe the communication process.
- Relate self-perception and behaviors to verbal and non-verbal communication.
- Recognize various meanings of verbal, vocal, and non-verbal symbols and their effect on interpersonal relationships.
- Describe conversations related skills, including in electronically mediated contexts.
- Identify methods of dealing with conflict in interpersonal relationships.

- List and describe effective techniques for communicating ideas and feelings.
- List and define guidelines for effective listening and responding techniques.
- Describe the nature and stages of relationships.
- Describe the interviewing process and related interpersonal skills
- Identify the process and procedures of decision-making in groups.
- Identify leadership styles
- Prepare and deliver an informative speech
- Prepare and deliver a persuasive speech

This student companion contains the following components:

Learning Objectives. Each chapter begins with a short list of objectives for that chapter. These are written in the form "After studying this chapter you should be able to...". The idea here is to give you an idea of what your instructor expects you to understand when the chapter is completed. Think of it as a list of your goals for that chapter. The sample test questions are based on these.

Interactive Chapter Outline. This is a detailed outline of the corresponding textbook chapter. It includes space for you to write your own notes. Use it as a guide to the organization of each chapter and to help you takes notes in class or while reading. Research suggests that students learn better if they can concentrate more on the concepts themselves and less on how they are organized when taking notes. The interactive outline provides the organizational structure, allowing you to concentrate on the individual terms and ideas.

Key Terms. A list of all terms highlighted and defined in the margins of the textbook is presented here. Space is provided for you to write in the definition, examples, or additional notes. Looking up and writing out the definitions of these terms is an excellent study aid and helps to build your vocabulary. Test questions often use these terms.

Exercises. One of the most important features of this companion is the selection of chapter exercises. These activities are designed to help you understand and apply the key ideas and concepts from each chapter. There are several different types of exercises. These include:

InfoTrac and Internet-based: These activities make use of technology, the Internet and *InfoTrac College Edition*, an Internet-based research resource you will find useful when seeking additional information on key concepts or when doing research for speeches or projects. This text contains all exercises found in the textbook as well as additional *Communicate! Using InfoTrac College Edition* and *Communicate! Using Technology* activities.

Observe and analyze journal activities: In selected locations throughout the textbook are the *Observe and Analyze Journal Activity* icons. These prompt you to complete a journal activity in this workbook. All the necessary journal forms are located in this text.

There are some more "traditional" exercises in each chapter as well.
Chapter Quiz Questions. True/false, multiple choice, and short essay questions are provided. These questions are designed to be similar to those you might encounter in an examination. Page references are provided in the answer key so you may check your work. If you think any of my answers are incorrect or my questions misleading, let me know. My students do!

Useful and Interesting Internet Links. At the end of each chapter I list several useful or interesting Internet links that are relevant to the material covered in that chapter. I have collected these over the years and have "borrowed" many form colleagues. Feel free to check them out. All links were accurate and current at the time of writing. If you find a "dead link", let me know.

Miscellaneous Resources. Some chapters include other materials in addition to those listed above. This is especially true in the Group Communication and Public Speaking chapters.

I hope this introduction proved useful to you. Please let me know what you think. Hopefully after taking this course, you will have a better idea of how to do that! But before you pick up your pen or log on to your e-mail account, remember, this is my first time doing anything like this. Be gentle.

Leonard Assante
Department of Communication
Volunteer State Community College
Gallatin, TN 37066
Len.Assante@vscc.cc.tn.us

Student Workbook

for Verderbers'

Communicate!

Tenth Edition

I

FOUNDATIONS OF COMMUNICATION

CHAPTER 1: Communication Perspective

Learning Objectives
After studying this chapter, you should be able to answer the following questions:
- What is the definition of communication?
- Why is communication effectiveness so important to you?
- How does the communication process work?
- What functions does communication serve?
- How do communication settings vary?
- Why should a communicator be concerned about diversity?
- What major ethical issues face communicators?
- What major ethical issues face communicators?
- What major ethical issues face communicators?
- What is the measure of communication competence?
- How can you improve your communication skills?

Interactive Chapter Outline

I. The Communication Process

    A. Definition of Communication

_____

_____

    B. Participants

_____

_____

    C. Context

_____

_____

    D. Messages

_____

_____

    E. Channels

_____

_____

F. Noise

_____

_____

G. Feedback

_____

_____

II. Communication in Our Lives
   A. Communication Functions

   _____

   _____

      1. _____

      2. _____

      3. _____

      4. _____

      5. _____

      6. _____

   B. Communication Settings

   _____

   _____

      1. _____

      2. _____

      3. _____

4

4. _____

III. Communication Principles
    A. Communication has Purpose

_____

_____

    B. Communication is Continuous

_____

_____

    C. Communication Messages vary in Conscious Encoding

_____

_____

    D. Communication is Relational

_____

_____

    E. Communication is Culturally Bound

_____

_____

    F. Communication has Ethical Implications

_____

_____

    G. Communication is Learned

_____

_____

IV. Increasing our Communication Competence
    A. Writing Goal Statements

_____

_____

Key Terms

communication (p. 6)

_____

_____

participants (p. 6)

_____

_____

context (p. 6)

_____

_____

physical context (p. 6)

_____

_____

social context (p. 6)

_____

_____

historical context (p. 7)

_____

_____

psychological context (p. 7)

_____

_____

cultural context (p. 8)

_____

_____

message (p. 8)

_____

6

meaning (p. 8)

symbols (p. 8)

encoding (p. 8)

decoding (p. 8)

channel (p. 9)

noise (p. 9)

external noises (p. 9)

internal noises (p. 9)

semantic noises (p. 9)

feedback (p. 9)

interpersonal communication settings (p. 13)

problem-solving group settings (p. 13)

public-speaking settings (p. 13)

electronically mediated communication settings (p. 13)

ernail (p. 13)

newsgroup (p. 14)

Internet chat (p. 14)

spontaneous expression (p.16)

8

scripted (p. 16)

_____

_____

constructed message (p. 16)

_____

_____

complimentary relationship (p. 17)

_____

_____

symmetrical relationship (p. 17)

_____

_____

cultural diversity (p. 18)

_____

_____

ethics (p. 19)

_____

_____

truthfulness & honesty (p. 20)

_____

_____

moral dilemma (p. 20)

_____

_____

integrity (p. 20)

_____

_____

fairness (p. 20)

_____

_____

respect (p. 20)

_____

_____

responsibility (p. 20)

_____

_____

communication competence (p. 21)

_____

_____

skills (p. 23)

_____

_____

Exercises
Journal Activities

Journal Activity 1.1 - Conversations (p. 11)

Think of two recent conversations you participated in, one that you thought went really well and one that you thought went poorly. Compare them. Using the form that follows, describe the context in which the conversations occurred, the participants, the rules that seemed to govern your behavior and that of the other participants, the messages that were used to create the meaning and, the channels used, any noise that interfered with communication, the feedback that was shared, and the result.

Journal Activity 1.1 Worksheet.   Name:_____

	Conversation that Went Well	Conversation that Went Poorly
Context		
Participants		
Rules		
Messages		
Channel		
Noise		
Feedback		
End Result		

Journal Activity 1.2 - Communication Functions (p. 12)

Using the worksheet that follows, keep a log of the various communication episodes you engage in today. Tonight, categorize each episode by one of the six functions it served. Each episode may serve more than one function. Were you surprised by the variety of communication you engaged in such a relatively short period?

12

Journal Activity 1.2 Worksheet.   Name:_____

Episode	Function
1.	
2.	
3.	
4.	
5.	
6.	
7.	
8.	
9.	
10.	
11.	
12.	
13.	
14.	

Journal Activity 1.3 – Use of Email (p. 14)

Do you use Email? Consider the mailing you have done over the last week. Using the worksheet that follows, classify the kinds of messages you have written (use such headings as letters to friends, inquiries to Web sites, questions to professors, and so forth). How many messages do you receive each day? What percentage of those do you reply to? Compare your email use to regular mail. How many letters (not bills, advertisements or solicitations) do you send or receive each day?

Journal Activity 1.3 Worksheet.   Name:_____

Email:
Kinds of messages written over the past week:

1.

2.

3.

4.

5.

How many messages do you receive each day? _____

Percentage that you reply to: _____

Email vs. regular mail:
How many letters do you send or receive each day?   Send: _____ Receive: _____

1.4 Using InfoTrac College Edition (p. 19). Cultural issues play an important role in global business. For example, in the airline industry gate agents, flight attendants and other service providers must be able to communicate effectively with people who come from different cultures and speak different languages. Using InfoTrac College Edition, you can find an interesting article on this subject. After typing in "Intercultural Communication" as the Subject Guide, locate the article "Plane Talk," by John Freivalds. Read what the airline industry is doing to make language learning a priority among flight attendants and pilots. How is this training working to achieve industry goals?

1.5 Using InfoTrac College Edition. The ability to communicate in complex ways is often seen as a key difference between humans and lower animals. Using InfoTrac College Edition, type in "human communication" as the subject guide and locate an article that contrasts human and animal communication. Then list what you perceive to be three key differences between animal and human communication.

1.6 Using the Web (p. 21). Interested in learning more about ethical dilemmas? Take a look at the Web site sponsored by the Markkula Center for Applied Ethics at Santa Clara University. This site, called Ethics Connection, is open to anyone but was designed with students in mind. It focuses on issues such as how to recognize ethical dilemmas and how to think through to resolutions. Issues covered include health care, social policy, business and technology, human rights, and everyday decision-making. The Ethics Connection: http://scuish.scu.edu/Ethics/

1.7 Using the Web. Using the links listed at the end of this chapter, browse through some of the sites devoted to the study and research of communication. Are you surprised by how many sites there are? About the amount of research being done in the field? About the different types of communication specialties? Pick any two sites and write a brief comparison essay. Focus on the content and organization of the two sites. What did you learn from your visits?

<u>1.8 Analyzing Feedback</u>. Keep a one-day log of all the feedback (verbal and nonverbal) you receive from others while communicating. Ask someone who knows you well to indicate the kinds of feedback you typically give him or her while they communicate with you. Analyze the similarities and differences in the feedback you give and receive.

<u>1.9 Diagram a Communication Event</u>. Using the model of communication presented on page 10 in your text, diagram a recent conversation you had. Who were the participants? What messages were sent? Using what channels? What feedback was given? Was there any noise present? In what context did the communication take place. Draw a diagram of the model and insert each answer in the correct location.

<u>1.10 Communication Settings</u>. After reviewing the four communication settings discussed on pages 12-15, identify the setting you feel you are most effective in and why you feel that way. Which setting are you least effective in? Why? Select one setting for improvement. What do you think you will need to do to improve in that area? At the end of the semester, review this question. Did you improve? Did you improve using the methods you thought you would use?

Chapter 1 Quiz Questions (answers and page references in Appendix)

True/False

1. Shared beliefs, values and norms that affect the behaviors of large groups of people are called "culture".

2. Selecting verbal symbols to stand for ideas and feelings is called decoding.

3. The route traveled by a message is called encoding.

4. The major criteria for determining communication competence are successful and concrete.

5. A salesperson giving reasons why you should purchase a product is an example of the influence function of communication.

Multiple Choice

1. If your lawyer gives you legal advice that you follow without question, the relationship between your lawyer and you would be
    a. interdependent
    b. symmetrical
    c. complementary
    d. ambiguous

2. The process of creating or sharing meaning is called
    a. communicating
    b. encoding
    c. transmitting
    d. decoding

3. At breakfast, you ask your roommate's advice on whether you should take chemistry or physics to meet your science requirement. That night, when you see your roommate, you say "I decided on chem." Your roommate's understanding of that message is explained by
    a. physical context
    b. historical context
    c. psychological context
    d. noise

4. If a person is thinking about the great time she had last night while listening to a class lecture, these thoughts would be considered
    a. encoding
    b. decoding
    c. feedback

  d. noise
  e. none of the above

5. Which of the following is considered an ethical question?
  a. Saul gives Maria a reward for finding his lost dog.
  b. Juan takes Leonard's book out of his bag.
  c. Cindy tells her friends she bought the food for lunch when in fact Amanda did.
  d. Joe punches Nick in the arm.

Essay

1. Explain how the different types of noise affect meaning.

2. Describe the six different parts of the communication process.

3. Describe how communication competence is measured. Provide at least one example.

Useful and Interesting Internet Links

http://www.natcom.org - the Internet home of the National Communication Association, the largest organization of communication students, researchers and teachers. This site previews some of the activities communication scholars engage in and offers a variety of links to other sources.

http://www.montana.edu/~wwwcommd/effectcomm.html - This site examines the roles of encoding and decoding in the communication process. By David Sharpe, Montana State University.

http://www2.vscc.cc.tn.us/tca/resources.htm#TeachingResources - The Tennessee Communication Association provides a series of links for general communication resources useful for both students and instructors. By David Warner, TCA Webmaster.

http://www.west.asu.edu/lehnerj/Comm_guide.htm - Paula Crossman provides guidance regarding where and how to locate the information you need to complete communication assignments.

http://www.cios.org - The Communication Institute for Online Scholarship provides discussion in a variety of current issues in the filed of communication, links to extensive resources and links designed especially for students.

CHAPTER 2: Perception of Self and Others

Learning Objectives

After studying this chapter, you should be able to answer the following questions:

- What is perception?
- How does the mind select, organize and interpret information?
- What is the self-concept and how is it formed?
- What is self-esteem and how is it developed?
- How do our self-concept and self-esteem affect our communication with others?
- What affects how we accurately perceive others?
- What are some methods for improving the accuracy of social perception?

Interactive Chapter Outline

I. The Perception Process

_____

_____

A. Attention and Selection

_____

_____

B. Organization of Stimuli

_____

_____

C. Interpretation of Stimuli

_____

_____

II. Perception of Self; Self-Concept and Self-Esteem

A. Forming and Maintaining Self-Concepts

_____

_____

B. Developing and Maintaining Self-Esteem

_____

_____

C. Accuracy of Self-Concept and Self-Esteem

_____

_____

D. Presenting Ourselves

_____

_____

E. Self-Concept, Self-Esteem, and Communication

_____

_____

F. Cultural and Gender Differences

_____

_____

III. Perception of Others

A. Physical Characteristics

_____

_____

B. Social Behaviors

_____

_____

C. Stereotyping

_____

_____

D. Emotional States

_____

_____

E. Improving Social Perception

_____

_____

Key Terms

perception (p. 30)

_____

_____

pattern (p. 31)

_____

_____

interpret (p. 31)

_____

_____

self-concept (p. 32)

_____

_____

self-esteem (p, 32)

_____

24

incongruence (p. 34)

self-fulfilling prophecies (p. 35)

role (p. 36)

uncertainty reduction theory (p. 38)

halo effect (p. 39)

stereotypes (p. 40)

prejudice (p. 40)

discrimination (p. 40)

racism, ethnocentrism, sexism, ageism, able-ism, & other "-isms" (p. 41) attributions (p. 44)

_____

_____

perception check (p. 45)

_____

_____

Exercises
Journal Activities

📖 Journal Activity 2.1 – Self-Perceptions (p. 33)

How do you see yourself? On the sheet that follows, list the skills, abilities, knowledge, competencies, and personality characteristics that describe how you see yourself. To generate this list, try completing the sentences: "I am skilled at…," "I have the ability to…," "I know things about…," "I am competent at doing…" and "One part of my personality is that I am…" over and over again. List as many characteristics in each category as you can think of. What you have developed is an inventory of your self-concept. Review each item on your list. Recall how you learned that you had that talent or characteristic. How does this review help you understand the material you are studying?

📖 Journal Activity 2.1 Worksheet   Name:_____

CATEGORY	HOW LEARNED
<u>Skills</u>	
<u>Abilities</u>	
<u>Knowledge</u>	
<u>Competencies</u>	
<u>Personality characteristics</u>	

📖 Journal Activity 2.2 – Other's Perceptions (p. 34)

How do others see you? Repeat the self-perception exercise, but this time use these statements: "Other people believe I am skilled at…," "Other people believe I have the ability to…," "Other people believe I know things about…," "Other people believe I am competent at doing …," and "One part of my personality is that other people believe I am…" Again, review the items on the list. Recall who told you about those talents and characteristics.

📖 Journal Activity 2.2 Worksheet   Name:_____

CATEGORY	WHO TOLD ME
<u>Skills</u>	
<u>Abilities</u>	
<u>Knowledge</u>	
<u>Competencies</u>	
<u>Personality characteristics</u>	

📖 Journal Activity 2.3 – Who Am I? (p. 35)

Compare your self-perception and others' perception lists from the previous two Journal Activities. How are these lists similar? Where are they different? Do you understand why they are different? Are your lists long or short? Why do you suppose that is? Reflect on how your own interpretations of your experiences and what others have told you about you have influenced your self-concept. Now organize the lists you created, perhaps finding a way to group characteristics. Use this information to write an essay titled "Who I am, and how I know this." If you wish, use the table below to help organize your thoughts.

CATEGORY	SELF-PERCEPTION	OTHER-PERCEPTION
Skills		
Abilities		
Knowledge		
Competencies		
Personality Characteristics		

📖 Journal Activity 2.4 – Monitor Your Enacted Roles (p. 37)

For three days keep a record of your roles in various activities and situations: for example, "Lunch at Taco Bell with my best friend" or "Meeting with my manager about vacation schedule." Use the log sheet that follows make photocopies if you need additional pages. Describe the roles and images you chose to project in each setting. At the conclusion of the three-day observation period, write an analysis of your self-monitoring. To what extent does your communication behavior differ and remain the same across situations? What factors in a situation seem to trigger certain behaviors in you? How satisfied are you with the images or "selves" you displayed in each situation? Where were you the most pleased? Least pleased?

Journal Activity 2.4 Worksheet   Name:_____

Enacted Roles Log Sheet

Day :

Activity/Situation	Role Enacted/Image Projected
1.	
2.	
3.	
4.	
5.	
6.	
7.	
8.	
9.	
10.	
11.	
12.	
13.	
14.	
15.	
16.	
17.	
18.	
19.	
20.	

2.5 Using InfoTrac College Edition (p. 38).
Some people believe "the greater the discrepancy between a person's own assessment of his or her interpersonal style and the perception of others, the greater will be that individual's reported psychological stress." What does research show? Using InfoTrac College Edition, look under the subject "Self-evaluation: Periodicals." See Amy Van Buren (1997), "Awareness of interpersonal style and self-evaluation, "*Journal of Social Psychology, 137*, p. 429. Can you find additional related studies?

2.6 Using the Web (p. 37).
The internet has numerous sites and pages devoted to material on self-concept and self-esteem. Some sites review research, others offer practical advice and opinions. One particularly provocative opinion is that of Dr. Richard O'Connor in his statement entitled "Self-Esteem: in a culture where winning is everything and losing is shameful." The key question he asks is whether self-esteem as a general construct is always helpful. What points does Dr. O'Connor make? How does his conclusion square with what you have observed? To open his statement, go to
http://www.pioneerthinking.com/esteem.html

2.7 Using the Web.
About.com's psychology section has a large selection of articles related to perception.
Go to http://psychology.about.com/science/psychology/cs/percep/index.htm and click on
"Perception online tutorials," then "Vision and Art" to learn about how artists use
elements of perception when creating art. Write a brief essay summarizing what you
have learned from the tutorial and relating it to the material discussed in Chapter 2 of
your text. Are you surprised that artists study perception and use what they have
learned when creating two-dimensional designs?

34

2.8   Accuracy and Inaccuracy in Perception.
Some perceptions are not always accurate. To test this idea, do the following activity.
Record your work on the worksheet that follows.
A. Observe several other students in your classes in an attempt to determine their
mood. Choose both students you know well as well as those you don't know.
B. Using the three-step process of perception as outlines in Chapter 2, do the following:
      1.   *Attend* and *select* stimuli. List what items you focused on.7
      2.   *Organize* the stimuli. Look for any patterns in behavior. What did you
          observe?
      3.   *Interpret* the stimuli. What conclusion have you come to concerning
          his/her mood?
C. Finally, check your perception. Ask the students you observed to confirm your
perception. Note the stimuli you observed and the conclusion you came to. Is each
student's mood what you thought it would be?

2.8 Accuracy and Inaccuracy in Perception Worksheet.   Name: _____

Stimuli	Patterns	Interpretation	Know/ Not Know?	Accurate?

2.9 Culture and Self-Esteem/Self-Concept.

Imagine you live in a culture which values age over youth and group over individual. In a brief essay, speculate as to how your life would be different than it is now. Are these differences positive, negative, both or neither? If you live in such a culture, reverse the assignment.

2.10 Knowledge of Self.
Read each of the following scenarios. Put yourself in each situation and answer the questions for each.

Situation: A friend and classmate asks if you want a copy of a stolen answer sheet he has for an upcoming exam in a different class. *How do you answer?*

Situation: Someone you are really attracted to has just asked you out to a party, but you had already agreed to do something with a friend that evening. *How do you answer?*

Questions:
1. What role did your self-concept play in your responses?

2. What role did others' possible impressions of your behavior play in your responses?

Chapter 2 Quiz Questions (answers and page references in Appendix)

True/False

1. Selecting, organizing and assigning meaning to information from your senses is called perception.

2. As you get ready for a job interview, you say to yourself, "I know I wont get this job," and you end up not getting it. This is an example of a self-fulfilling prophecy.

3. The three steps of the perception process are selection, retention and attention.

4. Self-concept and self-esteem are essentially the same.

5. It is possible to improve our perception.

Multiple Choice

1. Self-esteem is defined in your text as
    a. our overall evaluation of our competence and personal worthiness
    b. the list of characteristics that define who we are
    c. part of the self-perception process that never changes
    d. all of the above

2. Jim decides the flashing red light in his rear-view mirror means he must pull over to the side of the road. This is an example of
    a. selection
    b. attending
    c. interpretation
    d. roles
    e. stereotyping

3. The richer our self-concept
    a. the higher our self-esteem
    b. the lower our self-esteem
    c. the better we are at the selection phase of perception
    d. the better we know and understand who we are

4. Suppose you prepare a meal for several friends. One of them comments that you are a good cook. You ignore the message or reply, "It was nothing special, anyone could have made that meal." This is an example of
    a. self-fulfilling prophecy
    b. how we may distort self-perceptions by filtering messages
    c. a negative role
    d. halo effect

5. You just received your income tax refund. You are in a very good mood all day. As a result you tend to see other people and events in a more positive way than you might otherwise. This is an example of
      a. how emotional states influence our perception
      b. halo effect
      c. roles
      d. none of the above

Essay

1. Contrast self-perception and self-esteem

2. Describe how we can improve our perception ability. Offer at least one example.

Useful and Interesting Internet Links

http://www.adiosbarbie.com - This site looks at self-esteem by discussing the "Barbie image" and its effect on women and men.

http://www.parascope.com/articles/0397/sublim.htm - This link connects to an article on the impact of subliminal meanings on the perception process.

http://www.geocities.com/Heartland/Bluffs/5400/ - This site examines the process of formation of one's personal identity.

http://www.mentalhelp.net/psyhelp/chap7/chap71.htm - Material from the book *Psychological Self Help* by Clayton Tucker-Ladd helps the reader understand the roots of prejudice.

http://www.mentalhelp.net/psyhelp/chap14/chap14d.htm - Another set of material from Tucker Ladd's book looks at self-concept and self-esteem.

http://www.serve.com/shea/stereodf.htm - Many people seem to have stereotypical ideas concerning people of other cultures. Robert Shea looks at stereotypes of Americans held by people from other cultures.

http://psychology.about.com/science/psychology/cs/percep/index.htm – About .com's psychology section has a large selection of articles and links related to perception.

CHAPTER 3: Verbal Communication

Learning Objectives
After studying this chapter, you should be able to answer the following questions:
- What is the relationship between language and meaning?
- What is the difference between the denotative and the connotative meaning of words?
- How can you improve your language usage so that it is more precise, specific and concrete?
- How can you use the skills of dating and indexing generalizations to increase the accuracy of your messages?
- What happens when people use language that is inappropriate for the situation?
- How can you phrase messages so they are perceived as appropriate for the situation?

Interactive Chapter Outline

I. The Nature of Language

_____

_____

   A. Uses of Language

_____

_____

   B. Language and Meaning

_____

_____

   C. Meaning varies across Sub-Groups

_____

_____

II. Speaking more clearly

_____

_____

A. Specificity, Concreteness and Precision

_____

_____

_____

B. Dating Information

_____

_____

C. Indexing Generalizations

_____

_____

D. Cultural Differences

_____

_____

E. Gender Differences

_____

_____

III. Speaking Appropriately

_____

_____

A. Formality of Language

_____

42

_____

B. Jargon and Slang

_____

_____

C. Profanity and Vulgar Expressions

_____

_____

D. Sensitivity

_____

_____

E. Causes and Effects of Offensive Language

_____

_____

Key Terms

language (p. 52)

_____

_____

denotation (p. 53)

_____

_____

context (p. 53)

_____

_____

connotation (p. 54)

_____

_____

specific words (p. 56)

_____

_____

concrete words (p. 57)

_____

_____

precise words (p. 57)

_____

_____

brainstorming (p. 59)

_____

_____

dating information (p. 61)

_____

_____

generalizing (p. 61)

_____

_____

indexing (p. 61)

_____

_____

low-context cultures (p. 62)

_____

_____

44

high-context cultures (p. 62)

_____

_____

speaking appropriately (p. 65)

_____

_____

jargon (p. 65)

_____

_____

slang (p. 65)

_____

_____

Exercises
Journal Activities

Journal Activity 3.1 – Denotative Meanings (p. 53)

1. Compile a list of ten slang or "in" words. Discuss how the meanings you assign to these words differ from the meanings your parents or grandparents assign to them (for example, "He's bad!"). Use the worksheet on the next page to complete your work.

📖 Journal Activity 3.1 – Denotative Meanings Worksheet

Word	Your Meanings	Parents/Grandparents Meanings
1.		
2.		
3.		
4.		
5.		
6.		
7.		
8.		
9.		
10.		

2. Write your own definition of each of the following words; then go to a dictionary and see how closely your definition matches the dictionary's

building_____

_____

justice_____

_____

love_____

_____

ring_____

_____

success_____

_____

band_____

_____

glass_____

_____

peace_____

_____

freedom_____

_____

honor_____

_____

📖 Journal Activity 3.2 – Synonyms (p. 58)

One good way to increase specificity, concreteness, and precision is to play "synonyms." Think of a word, then list words that mean about the same thing. For example, synonyms for "happy" are *glad, joyful*, and *pleased*. When you have completed your list, refer to a book of synonyms, such as *Roget's Thesaurus*, to find other words. Then, using the worksheet that follows, write what you think is the meaning of each word, focusing on the shades of difference in meaning among the words. When you are done, look up each word, even those of which you are sure of the meaning. The goal of this exercise is to select the most specific, concrete, or precise word to express your idea.

Original Word: _____

List of Words with similar meaning and their definitions:

_____

_____

_____

_____

_____

_____

Additional words found using a book of synonyms and their definitions:

_____

_____

_____

_____

_____

_____

Which word is the most specific, concrete or precise for your intended meaning?

📖 Journal Activity 3.3 – Monitoring Your Use of Language (p. 69)

Tape record at least ten minutes of your conversation with a friend of family member. Talk about a subject that you hold strong views about: affirmative action, welfare, school levies, candidates for office, etc. Be sure to get permission from the other person before you tape. At first, you may feel self-conscious about having a recorder going. But as you get into the discussion, it is quite likely that you will be able to converse normally.

Play back the tape and take notes of sections where your language might have been clearer. Using these notes, write better expressions of your ideas for each section you noted by using more precise, specific, and concrete language and by dating and indexing generalizations.

Replay the tape. This time take notes on any racist, sexist, or biased expression that you used. Using these notes, write more appropriate expressions for the ones you used.

Using the page that follows, write a paragraph or two that describes what you have learned about your use of language from this experience.

Journal Activity 3.3 – Monitoring Your Use of Language Worksheet

Conversation time and date: _____

Conversation participants: _____

Conversation topic: _____

Areas of unclear language: _____

_____

_____

_____

Areas of sexist, racist or biased language: _____

_____

_____

_____

What have you learned?

_____

_____

_____

_____

_____

_____

_____

_____

_____

_____

3.4 Using InfoTrac College Edition (p. 67)

Although it is easy to spot sexism in language when someone uses a negative slang term to describe a person of the opposite sex, there are other ways language can be considered "sexist."

Using the InfoTrac College Edition subject guide, enter the search terms "sexism in language." Click on "Periodical references." See "Gender Issues in Advertising Language," Nancy Artz (1999). Focus on one of the issues discussed in the article. What is the significance of the examples presented? Why should people be concerned about this issue?

3.5 Using InfoTrac College Edition

It is interesting to observe how language use and word choice changes over time. Using the InfoTrac College Edition subject guide, attempt to find information on how language use and word choice has changed over time.   Were you able to find anything? Pick one reference you found and summarize the material. Were you surprised at what you found? What are some of the reasons for the changing use of words?

3.6 Using InfoTrac College Edition

Using InfoTrac College Edition, find and read the article "I love you man: Overt expression of affection in male-male interaction," by Mormon and Floyd. Summarize the article using the worksheet below, then develop guidelines for how men can use language to develop intimacy.

Article Summary:

Guidelines for Creating Intimacy Using Language:

3.7 Using Technology (p. 59)

How your ideas are worded can make a great deal of difference in whether people will understand or be influenced by what you say. You can use your word processing software to help you with your brainstorming. Nearly every word processing package has a thesaurus (a list of words and their synonyms) for the user to access. For instance, in the Microsoft Word package, the user can highlight a specific word, click on "Tools," drag down to "Thesaurus," and be presented with synonyms for the word. For practice, select any word that you would like to improve upon and look at the synonym choices available. Then select the choice you believe would be most meaningful. For instance, if you highlighted "difficult" when you clicked on Thesaurus, you would be shown *hard, laborious, arduous,* and *strenuous.* If you wanted more choices, you could then highlight one of these words to see additional choices. If you are trying to make the point that studying can be difficult, you might decide to use *arduous* as the most precise word.

3.8 Using the Web

The Internet also has language resources available. For example, go to http://www.britannica.com/dictionary. Brittanica.com offers access to a full dictionary with thesaurus. Simply enter the word you wish defined, and a menu of possible terms appears. Select one, and click on "Thesaurus" for synonyms. Try a few words using both an Internet-based thesaurus and either a word processor or bound version. Does each word you look up have the exact same list of synonyms in each type of thesaurus? If not, why do you suppose there are differences? Remember to consider language differences across cultures and times.

3.9 Language Use Across Cultures

Attend a religious or cultural service in a place of worship or gathering that is attended primarily by individuals whose race differs from yours. Do not take notes or otherwise appear disrespectful, but do observe the verbal communication of the individuals present. Look at both the leaders of the event and the participants. Afterwards, compare and contrast the verbal communication observed in this event and that seen in events or services you normally attend.

3.10 Analyzing Language

Analyze a political message (campaign ad, speech, interview, etc.) using the concepts of concreteness, precision and specificity of language. Could the message be more concrete, precise and/or specific? If so how? If so, do you think the language was purposefully less concrete, precise and/or specific than it could have been? Why?

Chapter 3 Quiz Questions (answers and page references in Appendix)

True/False

1. The text defines language as the body of words and the systems for their use that are common to the people of the same language community.

2. Denotative meanings are the standard dictionary meanings for words.

3. A word's meaning can be affected by other words in the same sentence.

4. Saying "split-level ranch" instead of "house" is an example of word concreteness.

5. Dating information is telling when the information was true.

Multiple Choice

1. Which of the following is NOT true of denotative meanings?
    a. meanings change over time
    b. meanings vary depending on life experiences
    c. there can be more than one denotative meaning for a word
    d. all of these are true
    e. none of these are true

2. Saying "A professor puts in long, hard years to earn his degree"
    a. is an example of word connotation
    b. is an example of word denotation
    c. may be an example of sexist language
    d. may be an example of concrete language

3. One of the best skills to use to avoid stereotyping is
    a. dating
    b. feedback
    c. denotation
    d. connotation
    e. indexing

4. In response to the statement "I don't think we should ask Niki to be on the team – smart kids make lousy athletes," you might use an indexing response such as
    a. although geniuses are usually weak, we don't know Niki is a genius
    b. we can still ask him to be on the team because he is our friend
    c. Its true Niki is smart, but we don't know if she is athletic too.
    d. Niki is not as smart as you think

5. Jargon
   a. is the characteristic idiom of a special group or activity
   b. is never appropriate
   c. is often useful for dating information
   d. is the same as slang
   e. none of the above

Essay

1. Discuss the differences between low-context cultures and high-context cultures.

2. Analyze the statement "women tend to use both more intensifiers and more hedges than men."

Useful and Interesting Internet Links

http://www.britannica.com/dictionary - Free online dictionary and thesaurus.

http://www.lawlib.uh.edu/guides/writ_4.html - Words Matter! by Rod Borlase discusses the care lawyers must take when choosing words in court. Both judges and juries can be influenced by word choice.

http://www.uws.edu.au/uws/uwsn/admin/eou/policies4.html - The nondiscriminatory language policy of the University of Western Sydney is an excellent example of both the rational for and implementation of language use guidelines.

http://writers.s-one.net.sg/weifeng/connotations.html - An examination of connotation and denotation. Concise and a bit philosophical in nature.

http://seattletimes.nwsource.com/news/local/html98/whit_19990311.html - This article from *The Seattle Times* examines the controversy a falsified racist letter caused at a community college. An excellent example of the impact of language on individuals and groups.

CHAPTER 4: Nonverbal Communication

Learning Objectives

After studying this chapter, you should be able to answer the following questions:

- What types of body motions have communication meaning?
- What is paralanguage?
- What are the elements of paralanguage, and how does each affect message meaning?
- How do clothing, touching behavior, and use of time affect self-presentation?
- How is communication affected by the use pf physical space?
- How do temperature, lighting, and color affect communication?
- What are three ways to improve the messages you communicate through your nonverbal behavior?

Interactive Chapter Outline

I. The Nature of Nonverbal Communication Behavior

_____

_____

II. Body Motions

_____

_____

   A. Eye Contact

_____

_____

   B. Facial Expression

_____

_____

   C. Gesture

_____

D. Posture

E. How Body Motions are Used

F. Cultural Variations

G. Gender Variations

III. Paralanguage

A. Vocal Characteristics

B. Vocal Interferences

IV. Self-Presentation

A. Clothing and Personal Grooming

_____

_____

B. Poise

_____

_____

C. Touch

_____

_____

D. Time

_____

_____

E. Cultural Variations

_____

_____

V. Communication through Management of your Environment

_____

_____

A. Space

_____

_____

B. Temperature, Lighting and Color

_____

_____

_____

C. Cultural Variations

_____

_____

Key Terms

Nonverbal communication (p.75)

_____

_____

kinesics *or* body motions (p. 75)

_____

_____

eye contact *or* gaze (p. 75)

_____

_____

facial expression (p. 76)

_____

_____

gestures (p. 76)

_____

_____

posture (p. 76)

_____

_____

sign language (p. 77)

_____

60

paralanguage (p. 79)

pitch (p. 80)

volume (p. 80)

rate (p. 80)

quality (p. 81)

vocal interferences (p. 81)

poise (p. 82)

touch (p. 83)

duration (p. 84)

activity (p. 84)

_____

_____

punctuality (p. 84)

_____

_____

territory (p. 87)

_____

_____

Exercises
Journal Activities

📖 Journal Activity 4.1 – Gender Variations in Body Motions (p. 80)

Find a place in the cafeteria or another public spot where you can observe the conversation of others. You are to observe the nonverbal behaviors of three dyads for at least five minutes each. First, observe the interaction of two men, then the interaction of two women, and finally, the interaction of a man and a woman. Using the Observation Tally Sheet provided here, record each participant's behavior and any other behavioral cues you note. Using these observation notes, review the material on male and female use of body motions. Did your observations confirm these trends? If they did not, develop an explanation about why they didn't, using the sheet that follows.

Nonverbal Behavior Observation Form: Body Motions

Dyad #1:

Behavior (frequency)	Participant 1 (sex: ___)			Participant 2 (sex: ___)		
Eye contact	High	Med	Low	High	Med	Low
Smiling	High	Med	Low	High	Med	Low
Forward lean of body	High	Med	Low	High	Med	Low
Touches or plays with hair	High	Med	Low	High	Med	Low
Touches or plays with clothes	High	Med	Low	High	Med	Low
Taps hand or fingers on surface	High	Med	Low	High	Med	Low
Arm position relative to body	High	Med	Low	High	Med	Low

Dyad #2:

Behavior (frequency)	Participant 1 (sex: ___)			Participant 2 (sex: ___)		
Eye contact	High	Med	Low	High	Med	Low
Smiling	High	Med	Low	High	Med	Low
Forward lean of body	High	Med	Low	High	Med	Low
Touches or plays with hair	High	Med	Low	High	Med	Low
Touches or plays with clothes	High	Med	Low	High	Med	Low
Taps hand or fingers on surface	High	Med	Low	High	Med	Low
Arm position relative to body	High	Med	Low	High	Med	Low

Dyad #3:

Behavior (frequency)	Participant 1 (sex: ___)			Participant 2 (sex: ___)		
Eye contact	High	Med	Low	High	Med	Low
Smiling	High	Med	Low	High	Med	Low
Forward lean of body	High	Med	Low	High	Med	Low
Touches or plays with hair	High	Med	Low	High	Med	Low
Touches or plays with clothes	High	Med	Low	High	Med	Low
Taps hand or fingers on surface	High	Med	Low	High	Med	Low
Arm position relative to body	High	Med	Low	High	Med	Low

Using these observation notes, review the material on male and female use of body motions. Did your observations confirm these trends? If they did not, develop an explanation about why they didn't:

📖 Journal Activity 4.2 – Vocal Interferences (p. 82)

Tape record yourself talking for several minutes about any subject. When you finish, estimate the number of vocal interferences you used. Then replay the tape and compare the actual number with your estimate. How close was your estimate? Wait a day or two and try it again. As your ear becomes trained, your estimates will be closer to the actual number. Keep a record of your improvement using the worksheet provided below. Now that you have raised your awareness, identify the vocal interference you use most frequently and work to reduce its use in your everyday conversation.

Vocal Interference Worksheet

	Date	Estimated Number	Actual Number	Difference
1.				
2.				
3.				
4.				
5.				
6.				
7.				
8.				
9.				
10.				

Most commonly used interference:

64

📖 Journal Activity 4.3 – Clothing Choices (p. 82)

Take an inventory of your wardrobe. Begin by dividing your clothes into three groups: those you wear for "special" dress-up occasions, those you wear for everyday activities such as school and work, and those you wear for leisure or "grubbing around." Counter the number of pants, shirts, blouses, skirts, dresses, belts and shoes that are in each category. Is your wardrobe "balanced," or do you have an overabundance of one type of clothing? Was it easy or difficult for you to categorize your wardrobe this way? If someone who did not know you were to peruse your closet and drawers, what would that person's impression of you be? Would it be accurate? Write your answers below.

📖 Journal Activity 4.4 – Cultural Differences in Self-Presentation (p. 82)

Interview or converse with two international students from different countries. Try to select students whose cultures differ from one another and from the culture with which you are most familiar. Develop a list of questions related to the self-presentation behaviors discussed in your text and record them in the space provided below and on the following page. Try to understand how people in the international student's country differ from you in their use of nonverbal self-presentation behaviors. Prepare to share what you have learned with your classmates.

Interview Questions and Answers

Interview Questions and Answers

Journal Activity 4.5 – Intruding on Personal Space (p. 87)

Find a crowded elevator. Get on it and face the back. Make direct eye contact with the person you are standing in front of. Note his or her reaction. On the return trip, introduce yourself to the person that is standing next to you and begin an animated conversation. Note the reaction of others around you. Get on an empty elevator and stand in the exact center. Do not move when others board. Note their reactions. Record your reactions below, and be prepared to share what you have observed with your classmates.

4.6 Using InfoTrac College Edition (p. 85)

Touching behavior can be perceived as a sign of comforting, affection, or harassment. Using the InfoTrac College Edition subject guide, enter the term "touch." Click on "periodical references." Then open "Just the right touch," Patrick McCormick (June 1999) for a discussion of touch as comforting. Under what circumstances is touch most comforting?

4.7 Using InfoTrac College Edition
It is interesting to observe how the meaning for nonverbal gestures can differ across cultures. Using the InfoTrac College Edition subject guide, attempt to find information on different meanings certain gestures have in different cultures.   Were you able to find anything? Pick one reference you found and summarize the material. Were you surprised at what you found? What lesson can be learned from your research?

4.8 Using Technology (p 81)
As you watch a videotape of a movie or a television program, select a segment where two people are talking with each other for a couple of minutes. The first time you watch, mute the audio (turn off the sound). Based on nonverbal behaviors alone, determine the climate of the conversation (Are the people flirting? In conflict? Discussing an issue? Kidding around?). What nonverbal behaviors and reactions led you that conclusion? Watch the video a second time, observing nonverbals but also listening to vocal variations in volume, pitch, and rate of speed. Do any of these vocal cues add to your assessment? Then watch it a third time, focusing on what the characters are saying. Now analyze the segment. What percentage of meaning came from nonverbal elements? What did you learn from this exercise?

4.9 Using the Internet

Using e-mail, chat room, discussion board or online instant messaging software, conduct a running conversation with a friend, classmate or other acquaintance. Do not use videoconferencing software. Be sure to discuss several issues, engaging in both serious and humorous interactions. Analyze the conversation and its outcomes. Were there any ambiguities or misunderstandings? Were there any moments when you could not tell if your partner was being funny, serious, sarcastic, or emotional? Were there any times when your partner could not tell your level of sarcasm, humor, or emotion? Were these problems resolved? If so, how? Would a face-to-face conversation have avoided some or all of these problems? Why?

4.10 What Would You Do? (p. 90)

Read the *What Would You Do: A Question of Ethics* scenario on page 90 of your text. Answer the following questions in the space provided here.

1. Analyze Barry's nonverbal behavior. What was he attempting to achieve?

2. How do you interpret Lisa's and Marquez's nonverbal reactions to Barry?

3. Was Barry's behavior ethically acceptable? Explain.

Chapter 4 Quiz Questions (answers and page references in Appendix)

True/False

1. Nonverbal cues provide minimal social meaning in interpersonal communication.

2. When Juanita uses her hands to show shape and size while saying "A bocce ball is about 6 inches in diameter," she is using body action as an illustrator.

3. When we know we want to be at a job interview on time, we are operating under the aspect of time management known as activity.

4. A person who sits in the same chair every class period illustrates territoriality.

5. When people are trying to figure out whether you are comfortable with what you are saying, they are likely to consider your eye contact.

Multiple Choice

1. Pitch
    a. is defined as highness or lowness of tone
    b. changes often accompany volume changes
    c. may be higher when someone is expressing nervousness
    d. all of the above

2. If Christopher pounds his fist on the table while he is telling Karin "Don't bother me right now," we can say Christopher is
    a. using body movement to mimic emotion
    b. using body movement to describe emotion
    c. using body movement to emphasize speech
    d. none of the above

3. Stylized nonverbal gestures that serve as substitutes for words are
    a. adapters
    b. emblems
    c. affect displays
    d. illustrators
    e. never used

4. Which of the following is an example of "paralanguage"?
    a. pointing at the cat
    b. moving the furniture around to improve communication
    c. saying one word in a sentence louder than the others
    d. ignoring the cat

5. You are driving a nail with a hammer. You accidentally hit your finger with the hammer. The look on your face in response to the hammer hitting your thumb would be
   a. an affect display
   b. an adapter
   c. an emblem
   d. a regulator
   e. a polychronic

Essay

1. Discuss some cultural variations in self-presentation

2. Discuss how vocal interferences can influence the perception you make on others.

Useful and Interesting Internet Links

http://www.unl.edu/casetudy/456/traci.htm - "Analysis of Cultural Communication and Proxemics," a paper by environmental design student Traci Olsen.

http://socpsych.lacollege.edu/nonverbal.html - Louisiana College's nonverbal communication research page has a list of links related to the field and a list of key nonverbal communication researchers.

http://www.csun.edu/~vcecn006/nonverb.htm - "Nonverbal Communication Helps Us Live" is devoted to a helpful review of the importance of nonverbal communication in everyday life.

http://www.religioustolerance.org/ther tou.htm – A different approach to the importance of touch is this essay on the possibility of touch having healing powers.

http://hg.women.com/homeandgarden/decor/transf/31feng21.htm - The art of "Feng Shui" is explained in this alternative look at the importance of management of the environment.

II

INTERPERSONAL COMMUNICATION

CHAPTER 5: Conversations

Learning Objectives

After studying this chapter, you should be able to answer the following questions:

- What is a conversation?
- How does a casual social conversation differ from a pragmatic problem-consideration conversation?
- What are conversational rules, and what are their distinguishing features?
- What is the cooperative principle?
- What are the maxims of the cooperative principle, and how does each apply to conversation?
- What are the skills associated with effective conversation?
- What guidelines regulate turn-taking behavior?
- What is conversational coherence, and how can it be achieved?
- Why is politeness important in conversation?
- What additional skills are important for electronically mediated communication?

Interactive Chapter Outline

I. Characteristics of Conversation

_____

_____

II. Types and Structures of Conversations

_____

_____

    A. Structure of casual social conversation

_____

_____

    B. Structure of pragmatic problem consideration conversation

_____

_____

_____

III. Rules of Conversations

_____

_____

   A. Characteristics of Rules

   _____

   _____

   B. Phrasing Rules

   _____

   _____

IV. Effective Conversations follow the Cooperative Principle

_____

_____

V. Skills of effective Face-to-Face Conversationalists

_____

_____

   A. Have quality information to present

   _____

   _____

   B. As an Initiator, ask Meaningful Questions

   _____

   _____

   C. As a Responder, Provide Free Information

   _____

   _____

D. Credit Sources

_____

_____

E. Balance Speaking and Listening

_____

_____

F. Practice Politeness

_____

_____

V. Skills of Effective Electronically Mediated Conversationalists

_____

_____

A. Conversing via E-Mail

_____

_____

B. Conversing via Newsgroups and Internet Chat

_____

_____

C. Cultural variations in Effective Conversation

_____

_____

Key Terms

conversation (p. 98)

_____

casual social conversations (p. 99)

_____

pragmatic problem-consideration conversations (p. 99)

_____

rules (p. 101)

_____

cooperative principle (p. 103)

_____

maxims (p. 103)

_____

quality maxim (p. 104)

_____

quantity maxim (p. 104)

_____

relevancy maxim (p. 104)

_____

manner maxim (p. 104)

_____

76

morality maxim (p. 104)

politeness maxim (p. 104)

free information (p. 107)

credit sources (p. 108)

politeness (p. 109)

positive face needs (p.110)

negative face needs (p. 110)

face-threatening acts (FTAs) (p. 110)

e-mail (p. 113)

newsgroup (p. 114)

_____

_____

Internet chat (p. 114)

_____

_____

lurking (p. 115)

_____

_____

flaming (p. 115)

_____

_____

FAQs (p. 115)

_____

_____

netiquette (p. 115)

_____

_____

Exercises
Journal Activities

Journal Activity 5.1 – Problem-Consideration Conversations (p. 101)

Identify two recent problem-consideration conversations you have had: one that was satisfying and one that was not. Try to recall exactly what was said. Write the scripts for these conversations in the space provided below. Then try to identify each of the five parts of a problem-consideration conversation. Were any parts missing? Retain these scripts for further use later.

📖 Journal Activity 5.1 – Problem-Consideration Conversations

Script for conversation #1 (Satisfying):

Journal Activity 5.1 – Problem-Consideration Conversations

Script for conversation #2 (Not satisfying):

📖 Journal Activity 5.1, part 2 – Conversational Maxims (p. 106)

Use the two conversation scripts prepared in the preceding exercise. Which of the conversation maxims were followed? If there were violations, what were these, and how did they affect the conversation? Can you identify specific conversational rules that were used? Which of these were complied with, which were violated? How does this analysis help you understand your satisfaction with the conversation?

📖 Journal Activity 5.2 – Conversational Variety (p. 107)

During the next three days, deliberately try to introduce greater variety in your conversations with others. How well are you able to develop and maintain such conversations? Are they more or les satisfying than conversations on weather, sports, and daily happenings? Why? Record your observations below.

📖 Journal Activity 5.3 – Using Politeness (p. 112)

Think about the last time you committed a face-threatening act (FTA). Try to reconstruct the situation. What did you say? – try to recall as specifically as possible the exact words you used.

Analyze your FTA in terms of familiarity and status, power, and risk. Did you have greater or lesser status? Did you have greater or lesser social power? Was the risk of hurting the person large or small? In light of you analysis, write three different ways that you could have made your request. Try one that uses positive face statement; try one that uses negative face statements; try one that combines positive and negative statements. Record your observations and analysis below. Record your three different requests on the following page.

📖 Journal Activity 5.3 (three statements)

Positive Face Statement:

Negative Face Statement:

Combined Positive and Negative Statement:

5.4 Using InfoTrac College Edition (p. 110)

Certainly one important aspect of politeness is courtesy. Using InfoTrac College Edition, under the subject "courtesy," click on Periodical references. Several of the articles listed lament a decline in civility. See, for instance, "Come on, kids, show some respect" Andrew Steven (1999). Try to get a perspective on such questions as "Does courtesy (politeness) really matter?" and "To what extent?"

5.5 Using InfoTrac College Edition

Research suggests that politeness is universal to all cultures. Research this idea using InfoTrac College Edition. You may want to start using the directions in exercise 5.4, then click on the "Link" tab to find related articles, or you may wish to start a new search. Select a reference that focuses on the universal nature of politeness and summarize your findings below. Consider the following questions in your summary: "What is meant by the universal nature of politeness?" and "How is politeness (courtesy) manifested in various cultures?"

5.6 Using Technology (p. 100)

Think of times that you've made a call outside your home using a wireless cell telephone. How do your conversations differ from those you have made on a wired phone? Are they longer? Shorter? More focused on pragmatic problem considerations than on casual social exchanges?

Why do you think this is true? What differences do you see in the etiquette of the way you handle such conversations in comparison to the way you would handle them if you were face to face? Check out the guidelines for cell phone etiquette at http://www.letstalk.com/promo/unclecell2.htm

5.7 Using the Web

Using a web search engine such as Yahoo (http://www.yahoo.com) or Dogpile (http://www.dogpile.com), search for references on "netiquette." List some of the key elements of netiquette below. Why were these guidelines adapted?

5.8 Using the Communicate! CD-ROM
Use your Communicate! CD-ROM to access the video scenario for Chapter 5. Click on the "In Action" feature, then click on "Susan and Sheila." As you watch Susan and Shelia talking, notice what each woman says and how they create this conversation together. Perform the following analysis. (You may write your answers below or directly on the screen the CD-ROM provides for you.)

1. What type of conversation is this?

2. Identify the conversational maxims that you observe each woman following.

3. Where do you see each woman using the specific skills for effective conversation?

When you have answered these questions, click on the "Done" button on the screen or turn to page 118 in your Communicate! text. Compare your analysis to that of the authors.

<u>5.9 What Would You Do? (p. 121)</u>
Read the *What Would You Do: A Question of Ethics* scenario on page 121 of your text.
Answer the following questions in the space provided here.

1. Have you ever talked with someone like John? Where did John go wrong in his
conversational skills? What should he have done differently?

2. What are the ethical implications of Louisa and the rest of the group sneaking out the
side door without saying anything to John? Defend your position.

<u>5.10 Thinking About Online Conversation (p. 115)</u>
Have you had experience with electronically mediated conversation? Compared to
face-to-face conversation, what is the greatest shortcoming of EM conversation? What
can you do to compensate of that shortcoming?

Chapter 5 Quiz Questions (answers and page references in Appendix)

True/False

1. Online conversations are essentially the same as face-to-face conversations.

2. A newsgroup is defined as an online interactive message exchange between two or more people.

3. Lurking is always a violation of Netiquette.

4. Maxims are conversational requirements.

5. One characteristic of rules is that are contextual –that they can apply in some situations but not others.

Multiple Choice

1. Social conversations differ from problem-consideration conversations in
    a. the kinds of topics discussed
    b. the goals of the conversation
    c. when the conversations occur
    d. all of the above

2. Jamie is talking to her friend Zack about classes for the next semester. She says "I think I'm going to take that Business and Professional Communication class in the fall. Jenny told me about and said it would be a good course." This is an example of:
    a. giving turn-taking cues
    b. the manner maxim
    c. crediting sources
    d. prescriptive rules
    e. none of the above

3. Saying to your professor "I can see that you're really busy right now, but I was wondering if you could answer a quick question" is an example of
    a. meeting someone's negative face needs
    b. meeting someone's positive face needs
    c. making a face-threatening act
    d. applied turn-taking rules

4. Face-threatening acts
    a. should be avoided at all times
    b. are normal
    c. can be used with positive politeness
    d. both b and c

5. Conversational rules
   a. are prescriptive in nature
   b. can tell us what to do or not to do in a situation
   c. allow for choice in behavior
   d. can vary from situation to situation
   e. all of the above

Essay

1. Discuss the four primary characteristics of rules. Include an example for each characteristic.

2. Describe why meaningful questions posed by an initiator should require more than a "yes" or "no" answer.

Useful and Interesting Internet Links

http://www.yahoo.com - The Yahoo Internet search engine is one of the most popular web destinations. Use it to search for information on any topic using a simple search engine. Also has links to various directories and information resources.

http://www.dogpile.com - The Dogpile search engine actually searches a list of other search engines for the topic or key words desired and returns results sorted by the search engine used.

http://www.hyperlexia.org/aha_about_conversation.html - "Learning about conversation" from the Center for Speech and Language Disorders, discusses rules of conversation as applied to children with learning and socializing disabilities.

http://teenmusic.about.com/teens/teenmusic/library/blchatrule.htm?iam=dpile&terms=%2Bconversation+%2Brules - About.com's teen music chat room has a set of rules and guidelines for electronically mediated conversation.

http://www.dcn.davis.ca.us/help/internet/netiquette.html - A Guide to Electronic Communication & Network Etiquette by Joan Gargano provides an extensive etiquette resource for electronically mediated communication.

http://goeurope.about.com/travel/goeurope/library/planner/blp_etiquette_countries.htm?iam=dpile&terms=%2Betiquette - An excellent guide to etiquette rules in various European countries, "Etiquette tips by Country" is a great way to learn about courtesy in different cultures.

CHAPTER 6: Listening

Learning Objectives

After studying this chapter, you should be able to answer the following questions:

- What are the five concepts involved in listening?
- How can you focus your attention?
- What is empathy?
- How can you ask questions to increase understanding?
- How can you paraphrase both the content and the intent of another's message?
- What are three devices for remembering information?
- How can you evaluate inferences?
- How can you make appropriate supporting statements?
- How can you give reasonable alternative interpretations of events?

Interactive Chapter Outline

I. Attending

_____

_____

II. Understanding

_____

_____

   A. Empathy

_____

_____

   B. Questioning

_____

_____

   C. Paraphrasing

_____

III. Remembering (Retaining Information)

    A. Repeat information

    B. Construct Mnemonics

    C. Take Notes

IV. Critical Analysis

V. Responding Empathetically to give Comfort

    A. Supporting

B. Interpreting

_____

_____

_____

Key Terms

listening (p. 126)

_____

_____

attending (p. 126)

_____

_____

understanding (p. 127)

_____

_____

empathy (p. 128)

_____

_____

empathic responsiveness (p. 128)

_____

_____

perspective taking (p. 128)

_____

_____

sympathetic responsiveness (p. 128)

_____

_____

respect (p. 128)

_____

_____

questioning (p. 130)

_____

_____

paraphrasing (p. 132)

_____

_____

content paraphrase (p. 132)

_____

_____

feelings paraphrase (p. 132)

_____

_____

remembering (p. 134)

_____

_____

mnemonic device (p. 135)

_____

_____

critical analysis (p. 137)

_____

_____

inferences (p. 137)

_____

_____

comforting (p. 139)

_____

_____

supporting responses (p. 141)

_____

_____

interpreting responses (p. 144)

_____

_____

Exercises
Journal Activities

📖 Journal Activity 6.1 -- Attending (p. 127)

Select an information-oriented program on your public television station (such as *NOVA, News Hour with Jim Lehrer*, or *Wall Street Week*). Watch at least fifteen minutes of the show while lounging in a comfortable chair or while stretched out on the floor with music playing on a radio in the background. For the next fifteen minutes, make a conscious effort to use the guidelines for increasing attentiveness. Then contrast your listening behaviors. What differences did you note between the second segment and the first? What were the results of those differences?

Scenario 1 notes:	Scenario 2 notes:

📖 Journal Activity 6.1 (cont.)

Use the space below to write an essay that answers the questions posed in Activity 6.1 above.

📖 Journal Activity 6.2 – Empathizing Effectively (p. 129)

Describe the last time you effectively empathized with another person. Write a short analysis below. Be sure to cover the following: What was the person's emotional state? How did you recognize it? What were the nonverbal cues? Verbal cues? What type of relationship do you have with this person? How similar is this person to you? Have you ever had a real or vicarious experience similar to the one the person was reporting?

📖 Journal Activity 6.3 – Creating Mnemonics (p. 135)

Mnemonics are useful memory aids. Using the space provided below, construct a mnemonic for the five phases of the listening process identified in Chapter 6 of your text: attending, understanding, remembering, evaluating, and responding. Write down your mnemonic.

Tomorrow, while you are getting dressed, see whether you can recall the mnemonic you created. Then see whether you can recall the phases of the listening process from the cues in your mnemonic. How well did you do? Be prepared to share what you wrote with your classmates.

6.4 Using InfoTrac College Edition (p. 126)

Why is listening perceived to be important in so many professions? Using InfoTrac College Edition, under the subject of "listening," click on Periodical references. To answer the question, open articles such as Sandra Hagevik, "Just Listening" (1999) and Sheila C. Bentley "Listening Better: A Guide to Improving What Might Be the Ultimate Staff Skill (1998). Which specific listening skills seem to be agreed upon as most important?

6.5 Using InfoTrac College Edition

Refer back to the subject "listening" in InfoTrac College Edition. Another way to tell that listening is important in a variety of fields and professions is to examine the variety of periodicals that include articles related to listening. Click on Periodical references and count the number of different periodicals represented. Note the variety of fields and professions represented. Click on a few different periodical references and examine the content of the articles. Can you find any similarities in how listening is discussed across disciplines? What do you think explains this?

6.6 Using Technology (p. 135)

Speakerphones, wireless phones, and cellular phones have brought a new level of convenience to communication. These days you can work on your computer, drive, or even cook dinner while you are on the phone. But what effects have these devices had on your listening effectiveness? Next time you are using one of these devices, be conscious of your listening. How well are you doing at attending, understanding and remembering? Which of the guidelines provided in this chapter should you apply to improve your listening under these conditions?

6.7 Using the Web

Using the "Dogpile" search engine listed in the Chapter 5 "Useful and Interesting Internet Links" section (http://www.dogpile.com), conduct a web search using the subject "listening skills". Find the entry "Empathy and Listening Skills" entry. Click on the link to go to the "Empathy and Listening Skills Home Page" by Dr. Lawrence Bookbinder. Read the sample conversations and write a short essay on the importance of listening and empathy for relationship building. Also, what is a "psychological hug?"

6.8 What would you do? (p. 148)
Read the *What Would You Do: A Question of Ethics* scenario on page 148 of your text.
Answer the following questions in the space provided here.

1. How ethical was Janeen's means of dealing with her dilemma of not wanting to talk
on the phone but not wanting to hurt Barbara's feelings?

2. Identify ways in which both Janeen and Barbara could have used better and perhaps
more ethical interpersonal communication skills. Rewrite the scenario incorporating
these changes.

6.9 <u>Using the Communicate! CD-ROM (p. 148)</u>
Use your Communicate! CD-ROM to access the video scenario for Chapter 6. Click on the "In Action" feature, then click on "Listening." As you watch Damien and Chris discuss Chris's recent problem at work, focus on Damien's use of listening skills. Perform the following analysis. (You may write your answers below or directly on the screen the CD-ROM provides for you.)

1. What does Damien do that shows he is attending?

2. What does he do that demonstrates his understanding?

3. Does he use critical listening to separate facts from inferences?

4. How does he show empathy?

(When you have answered these questions, click on the "Done" button on the screen to compare your analysis to that of the authors.)

6.10 Thinking about Comforting Responses (p. 145)

Think of the last time you told someone about an event or circumstance in which you felt scared, hurt, disappointed, or angry. Did the person try to comfort you? If so, report what was said. Did the person try to offer alternative interpretations for what had happened? Did this help you? If so, how? If not, why not? What can you learn from this experience that will help you improve your response skills?

Chapter 6 Quiz Questions (answers and page references in Appendix)

True/False

1. Questions should be phrased as complete sentences/

2. Listening involves noting verbal cues only.

3. Saying something over three or four times until you remember it is an example of a mnemonic.

4. Inferences are never true.

5. Brant Burleson is a noted scholar in the area of comforting behavior.

Multiple Choice

1. "The process of receiving, attending to, and assigning meaning to aural and visual stimuli" is the definition of
    a. listening
    b. critical analysis
    c. empathy
    d. inference making

2. Physical posture
    a. is irrelevant to listening
    b. guarantees successful listening
    c. is part of being prepared both mentally and physically to listen
    d. is only part of assigning meaning to information
    e. none of the above

3. Heather tells Sara that her boyfriend Stu is angry with her. Sara senses the sadness Heather is feeling and experiences a similar feeling of sadness. Sara's reaction is an example of
    a. perspective taking
    b. empathetic responsiveness
    c. sympathetic responsiveness
    d. respect

4. Fred says "Man, I really blew that assignment, I guess I'm just not cut out for physics!" Barney replies "If I understand you right, you didn't do a good job on last night's homework?" Barney is using what strategy of improving understanding?
    a. empathy
    b. questioning
    c. attending

    d. paraphrasing
    e. articulating

5. Michelle remembers phone numbers by visualizing how her fingers move across the dial pad, even to the extent of pretending to "dial" a phone number in air. This artificial memory aid is an example of
    a. inference making
    b. a mnemonic device
    c. a selection device
    d. critical analysis
    e. supporting behavior

Essay

1. Describe the different stages of the listening process.

2. Describe three ways to improve your ability to remember information.

Useful and Interesting Internet Links

http://www.csbsju.edu/academicadvising/help/eff-list.html - College of Saint Benedict | Saint John's University study skills guide for effective listening in class

http://www.listen.org/pages/quotes.html - The International Listening Association's list of quotes about listening. The association's home page is http://www.listen.org/.

http://www.itmweb.com/essay514.htm - Kenneth Johnson's essay on the importance of effective listening and skills you can use to improve your listening ability.

http://userpages.umbc.edu/~cweide1/oraloutline.html - "Barriers to Effective Listening" by Jack E. Hulbert.

http://marriage.about.com/people/marriage/cs/listening/index.htm?iam=dpile&terms=%2Beffective+%2Blistening - This sit explores the importance of listening in marriage.

http://www.vandruff.com/art_converse.html - "Conversational Terrorism" is a humorous approach to a discussion of what not to do when responding to others.

CHAPTER 7: Self-Disclosure and Feedback

Learning Objectives
After studying this chapter, you should be able to answer the following questions:

- What do we mean by self-disclosure?
- What are the guidelines for disclosing?
- When and how does one describe feelings?
- What are the differences between displaying feelings and describing feelings?
- What are the differences between passive, aggressive, and assertive responses?
- How can you assert yourself appropriately?
- What can you do to improve giving praise and constructive criticism?

Interactive Chapter Outline

I. Self-Disclosure

_____

_____

A. Guidelines for Appropriate Self-Disclosure

_____

_____

B. Cultural and Gender Differences

_____

_____

II. Disclosing Feelings

_____

_____

A. Withholding or Masking Feelings

_____

_____

B. Displaying Feelings

_____

_____

C. Describing Feelings

_____

_____

III. Owning Feelings

_____

_____

IV. Giving Personal Feedback

_____

_____

A. Praising

_____

_____

B. Giving Constructive Criticism

_____

_____

V. Assertiveness

_____

_____

A. Contrasting Methods of Expressing our Needs and Rights

_____

_____

B. Distinguishing Between Passive, Aggressive and Assertive Responses

Passive: _____

_____

Aggressive: _____

_____

Assertive: _____

_____

C. Cultural Variations

_____

_____

Key Terms

self-disclosure (p. 156)

_____

_____

report-talk (p. 160)

_____

_____

rapport-talk (p. 160)

_____

_____

withholding feelings (p. 161)

_____

_____

displaying feelings (p. 161)

_____

_____

describing feelings (p. 162)

_____

_____

owning feelings or opinions (p. 167)

_____

_____

praising (p. 169)

_____

_____

constructive criticism (p. 170)

_____

_____

assertive behavior (p. 172)

_____

_____

passive behavior (p. 172)

_____

_____

aggressive behavior (p. 172)

_____

_____

Exercises
Journal Activities

📖 Journal Activity 7.1 – Expressing Criticism (p. 170)
Think about the last time you criticized someone's behavior. Answer the following questions in the space provided below: Which, if any, of the guidelines for constructive feedback did you follow or violate? If you were to do it again, what would you say differently?

📖 Journal Activity 7.2 – Passive, Aggressive and Assertive Behavior (p. 173)

For the next day or two, observe people and their behavior. Take note of situations where you believe people behaved in passive, aggressive, and assertive ways. Then, in the space provided below, answer the following questions:

Which of the ways seemed to help the people achieve what they wanted?

Which of the ways seemed to maintain or even improve their interpersonal relationship with the other person or other people?

110

📖 Journal Activity 7.3 – Learning to Respond Assertively (p. 176)
Identify five situations in the past where you were nonassertive or aggressive. In the space provided below, write the dialog for each situation. Then substitute an assertive response for the aggressive or nonassertive reactions you expressed in each case.

Situation 1:

Situation 2:

Situation 3:

Situation 4:

Situation 5:

7.4 Using InfoTrac College Edition (p. 175)

As we have seen, assertiveness is sometimes perceived as aggressiveness. Using the InfoTrac College Edition subject guide, enter the term "Assertiveness." Click on "Assertiveness (Psychological)." Look for articles that offer guidelines for being assertive, such as "How to Assert Yourself" by Kathiann Kowalski (1998), an article that considers the importance of behaving assertively without becoming aggressive. Summarize the article's main ideas here.

7.5 Using InfoTrac College Edition

Are males really more aggressive than females on average? Are there cultural differences in what constitutes assertive behavior? Using InfoTrac College Edition, try to determine what the research suggests. Using the subject guide, again enter "assertive" and locate references that focus on differences across cultures. What did you find? Summarize your results below.

7.6 Using Technology (p. 159)

Sign on to an online chat room. Spend at least five minutes just "lurking" (listening). Then begin to participate in the chat. Considering both your comments and those with whom you are "chatting," how do the levels of self-disclosure differ from in-person conversations? Is there really much self-disclosure occurring? If so, how doe sit compare to self-disclosure in face-to-face encounters? How can you tell if the disclosures are truthful? Use the space below to record your observations.

(If you need an introduction to chat rooms and how to get started, enter Yahoo! Chatrooms, click on "search," and then click on "People connection chat." http://www.yahoo.com)

Chat room entered: _____

<u>7.7 What would you do? (p. 178)</u>
Read the *What Would You Do: A Question of Ethics* scenario on page 178 of your text. Answer the following questions in the space provided here.

1. What are the ethical issues in this case?

2. Did Maria behave ethically in this situation?

3. If you were one of the women advising Maria, what would you recommend that she do?

7.8 Using the Communicate! CD-ROM (p. 178)

Use your Communicate! CD-ROM to access the video scenario for Chapter 7. Click on the "In Action" feature, then click on "Sharing Feelings." As you watch Trevor and Meg discuss the future of their relationship, focus on how effectively they are communicating. Answer each of the following questions below or in the spaces provided on the "Analysis" screen. When finished, click the "Done" button to compare your analysis to that of the authors. How do they compare?

1. How do Trevor and Meg disclose their feelings?

2. Note how effective each is at owning feelings and opinions.

3. How well do Trevor and Meg use praise and constructive criticism?

4. Notice how each demonstrates the characteristics of assertive behavior.

5. What is really Meg's fear?

7.9 Thinking About Communicating Your Feelings (p. 162)

Think back over the events of the day. At any time during the day did you feel particularly happy, angry, disappointed, excited or sad? How did you communicate your feelings to others? Under what circumstances, if any, did you describe your feelings? What appear to be your most common ways of displaying (expressing) your feelings? Discuss what you might do to make sharing your feelings more interpersonally effective.

7.10 Thinking About The Vocabulary of Emotions (p. 163)

Look at each word listed below, say "I feel . . . ," and try to identify the feeling this word would describe. Write the words used to describe these feelings under the original word. Now turn to page 164 in your <u>Communicate!</u> text. Compare your list of words to the list in the book. How similar are they? Which of these words (from either list) are meaningful enough to you that you could use them to help you communicate your feelings? Circle those words.

Angry

Helpful

Loving

Embarrassed

Surprised

Fearful

Disgusted

Chapter 7 Quiz Questions (answers and page references in Appendix)

True/False

1. Assertiveness and Aggressiveness are synonymous.

2. Passive behavior is best for maintaining and improving interpersonal relationships.

3. You should always try to increase the level of self-disclosure in interpersonal relationships even if the other person does not.

4. It is best to ask permission before providing constructive criticism.

5. Some people belong to cultural groups that feel it is appropriate to mask feelings.

Multiple Choice

1. Megan tells Emily that she dated Travis for a while, but she stopped when she decided his only interest in her seemed to be sexual. Megan's statement could be classified as:
   a. description of feelings
   b. self-disclosure
   c. expression of feelings
   d. passive behavior
   e. aggressive behavior

2. When in the earlier stages of a relationship, it probably is a good idea to:
   a. not self-disclose any information during your first meeting
   b. disclose information only if asked to by the other person
   c. reveal the kind of information about yourself that you want the other person to disclose to you.
   d. only disclose feelings

3. You are reviewing another student's paper. The best way to open your criticism would be:
   a. Your first paragraph is great, but some of the other paragraphs are disorganized
   b. The paper is disorganized
   c. There are many problems here, but I think we can fix them.
   d. It's ok, but...
   e. None of the above are acceptable starts to constructive criticism

4. Saul is looking over his exam. He finds a mistake in his professor's addition of his total score. If Saul behaves assertively, which of the following does he say to his professor?
   a. You made a mistake. I get 7 more points.

b. Would you go over my test again?

c. I'm really mad at the way you counted my points wrong!

d. When I counted my point total, it came to 89, four more than the total on the exam cover. Am I correct?

5. You know that someone made a mistake that impacts you, but you say nothing. This is illustrative of:

a. assertive behavior

b. aggressive behavior

c. passive behavior

d. precision

e. none of the above

Essay

1. Discuss the differences between assertive, passive and aggressive behaviors.

2. Describe what it means to "maintain ownership of your feelings" when being assertive.

Useful and Interesting Internet Links

http://www.mhnet.org/psyhelp/chap13/chap13i.htm - Psychological Self Help offers a tutorial on how to overcome the fear of self-disclosure many people have.

http://www.mhnet.org/psyhelp/chap13/chap13j.htm - This site continues the discussion found in the first site above.

http://mentalhealth.about.com/health/mentalhealth/library/archives/1299/blboysfeelings.htm?iam=dpile&terms=%2Bself+%2Bdisclosure - Although it has a LONG address, this site contains an interesting article that explores the reasons why boys do not self-disclose feelings.

http://www.minoritycareernet.com/newsltrs/96q2give.html - A concise list of hints for giving constructive criticism.

http://artistexchange.about.com/hobbies/artistexchange/library/weekly/aa031601a.htm?iam=dpile&terms=%2Bconstructive+%2Bcriticism - A look at criticism from an artist's perspective. This essay also deals with how to handle criticism when it is directed at you.

CHAPTER 8: Communicating in Relationships

Learning Objectives

After studying this chapter, you should be able to answer the following questions:

- What are the major types of relationships?
- What are effective ways of starting a relationship?
- How are relationships built online?
- How are the skills of descriptiveness, openness, provisionalism, and equality used in maintaining relationships?
- What does interpersonal needs theory tell us about relationships?
- What does exchange theory tell us about relationships?
- What is conflict, and why does it occur in relationships?
- What are the five conflict styles, and when is each style appropriate?
- What skills are used to initiate conflict effectively?
- What skills are used in responding to a conflict initiated by another?

Interactive Chapter Outline

I. Types of Relationships

_____

_____

   A. Acquaintances

_____

_____

   B. Friends

_____

_____

   C. Close Friendships or Intimates

_____

_____

II. Communication in the Stages of Relationships

_____

_____

   A. Starting or Building Relationships

_____

_____

   B. Examining Disclosure and Feedback Ratios in Relationships

_____

_____

   C. Stabilizing Relationships

_____

_____

   D. Relationship Disintegration

_____

_____

III. Role of Electronic Communication in Building Relationships

_____

_____

   A. Development of Electronically Mediated Relationships

_____

_____

   B. From Online to In-Person Relationships

_____

_____

   C. The Dark Side of Electronically Mediated Relationships

_____

_____

IV. Theoretical Perspectives on Relationships

_____

_____

    A. Interpersonal Needs Theory

_____

_____

    B. Exchange Theory

_____

_____

V. Conflict

_____

_____

    A. Styles of Managing Conflict

_____

_____

        1. Withdrawing

_____

_____

        2. Accommodating

_____

_____

        3. Forcing

_____

_____

4. Compromising

_____

_____

5. Collaborating

_____

_____

VI. Communication Skills for Resolving Conflicts through Collaboration

    A. Initiating Conflict Appropriately

_____

_____

    B. Responding to Conflict Effectively

_____

_____

    C. Learning for Conflict-Management Failures

_____

_____

Key Terms

good relationship (p. 186)

_____

_____

acquaintances (p. 186)

_____

_____

friends (p. 186)

_____

_____

trust (p, 187)

_____

_____

close friends or intimates (p. 188)

_____

_____

passive strategy (p. 188)

_____

_____

active strategy (p. 188)

_____

_____

interactive strategy (p. 188)

_____

_____

idea-exchange communication (p. 189)

_____

_____

gossip (p. 189)

_____

_____

self-disclosure (p. 190)

_____

_____

feedback (p. 190)

_____

_____

johari window (p. 190)

_____

_____

stabilization (p. 193)

_____

_____

speaking descriptively (p. 193)

_____

_____

speaking openly (p. 193)

_____

_____

speaking tentatively (p. 193)

_____

_____

speaking equally (p. 194)

_____

_____

technological addictions (p. 198)

_____

_____

interpersonal needs theory (p. 199)

_____

_____

affection need (p. 199)

_____

inclusion need (p. 199)

control need (p. 200)

exchange theory (p. 200)

rewards (p. 200)

costs (p. 200)

interpersonal conflict (p. 201)

withdrawal (p. 202)

mulling (p. 202)

accommodating (p. 203)

_____

forcing (p. 203)

_____

_____

compromising (p. 204)

_____

_____

collaborating (p. 204)

_____

_____

Exercises
Journal Activities

📖 Journal Activity 8.1 – Friends and Acquaintances (p. 190)

In the spaces provide below:

1. Identify five people you consider to be your friends. In what kind of context did you first meet? What attracted you to them? What aspects of attraction have proved to be the most important as the relationships developed?

	Friend	Context	Attraction Then	Attraction Now
1.				
2.				
3.				
4.				
5.				

📖 Journal Activity 8.1 – Friends and Acquaintances (cont.)

2. Identify five people you consider to be acquaintances. List the ways in which communication with your acquaintances differs from communication with your friends.

Acquaintances	How Communication Differs w/Friends
1.	
2.	
3.	
4.	
5.	

3. What would you need to happen in order for those people you listed as acquaintances to become friends?

📖 Journal Activity 8.2 – Positive and Negative Climates (p. 195)

Think of two recent interactions you have had. Choose one that was characterized by a positive communication climate and one that was characterized by a negative communication climate. Recall as best you can some of the specific conversation from each interaction. In the space provided below, write down each conversation like a script. Now analyze each script. Count specific instances of being descriptive and giving evaluation. Recall whether hidden agendas were evidenced. Count instances of provisional wordings and of dogmatic wordings. Look for instances where equality of interactants was present and instances where one person spoke in a way that conveyed an attitude of superiority. Discuss your results. How much did using or failing to use the four skills presented in this section contribute to the climate you experienced?

Script of Interaction #1:

Journal Activity 8.2 – Positive and Negative Climates (cont.)

Script of Interaction #2:

📖 Journal Activity 8.2 – Positive and Negative Climates (cont.)

Analysis and Discussion: (Answer the questions listed above here.)

📖 Journal Activity 8.3 – Conflict Episodes (p. 207)

In the space proved below, describe a conflict episode you have recently experienced. How did you and the other person behave? What was the outcome of the conflict? How did you feel about it then? Now? Could the conflict have been handled in a different way that could have resulted in a better outcome?

📖 Journal Activity 8.4 – Conflict Failures (p. 211)

Think of a recent conflict you experienced in which the conflict was not successfully resolved. Analyze what happened using the concepts from this chapter. Answer the following questions in the space provided below. What type of conflict was this? What style did you adopt? What was the other person's style? How did styles contribute to what happened? How well did your behavior match the guidelines recommended for initiating and responding to the conflict? How might you change what you did if you could "redo" this conflict episode?

8.5 Using InfoTrac College Edition (p. 193)

How do college students deal with conflict? Using the InfoTrac College Edition subject guide, enter the term "interpersonal conflict." Check the periodical references under Interpersonal Conflict. You'll find articles that look at conflict in a variety of settings such as marriage, family structure, children's adjustment, and so on. See Marianne Bell and David Forde's article "A factorial survey of interpersonal conflict resolution" in the *Journal of Social Psychology*. Does the behavior described in this article fit you? Do any of the research findings surprise you? Why?

8.6 Using InfoTrac College Edition

How does online education impact the relationship between students and teachers? Many students and teachers feel the relationship developed in a classroom setting is very important to educational success. So what happens when that face-to-face relationship is replaced with an online one? Using the InfoTrac College Edition subject guide, enter the term "online relationship." See Joan E. Thiele, Carol Allen and Mary Stucky's article "Effects of web-based instruction on learning behaviors of undergraduate and graduate students" in *Nursing and Health Care Perspectives*. Summarize the article in the space provided below. What did the authors find? Are you surprised? Why?

8.7 Using the Web

Select one of the web sites noted at the end of this chapter. Each one is indicative of the hundreds of web sites dealing with the material from this chapter. Review the site and summarize the content in the space below. Compare this material to that found in your text. What are the similarities and/or differences between the web page and the text material? Attempt to explain any differences you might find.

8.8 Using Technology (p. 188)

Record a portion of a movie or TV program in which friends are having a conversation. Analyze it on the basis of expectations of friendships, including positiveness (enjoyment of talking with each other), assurance, openness, networking, and task sharing. Which of these factors seem evident in the conversation? What other elements were shown in the conversation? Did these seem to contribute to or detract from the relationships? In what ways is this conversation typical or atypical of those you have had with your friends? Explain.

8.9 Using the Communicate! CD-ROM (p. 213)
Use your Communicate! CD-ROM to access the video scenario for Chapter 8. Click on the "In Action" feature, and then click on "Communication in Relationships." As you watch Jan and Ken's conversation, focus on how the nature of their relationship influences their interaction. Click to "submit" your answers and compare to the authors' response.

1. What does each person do to maintain the relationship?

2. How does each person handle this conflict?

3. How well does each person listen to the other?

4. Are Jan and Ken appropriately assertive?

5. Notice how well each provides feedback and describes feelings.

8.10 What Would You Do? (p. 212)
Read the *What Would You Do: A Question of Ethics* scenario on page 212 of your text. Answer the following questions in the space provided here.

1. Sort out the ethical issues in this case. Under which ethical guidelines would Sally's, Ed's, and Jamie's actions be considered ethical or unethical?

2. Using guidelines from Chapter Eight in the text, role-play different key moments in this scenario, changing them to improve the communication ethics and outcome of the situation.

Chapter 8 Quiz Questions (answers and page references in Appendix)

True/False

1. Avoiding conflict and preventing conflict are the same thing.

2. Each of the five styles of conflict may be appropriate in some situations.

3. We engage in three communication activities to start and build relationships: striking up a conversation, keeping the conversation going and moving toward intimacy.

4. The johari window is a tool used to examine the relationship between disclosure and conflict.

5. There is no room for speaking tentatively when attempting to prevent conflict.

Multiple Choice

1. When you risk putting your well being in the hands of another, you are showing
   a. commitment
   b. trust
   c. self-disclosure
   d. idea-exchange behaviors
   e. none of the above

2. Exchange theory says people want relationships
   a. that yield high reward and low cost
   b. that yield high cost and low reward
   c. that provide affection, inclusion and control
   d. regardless of costs and rewards

3. Interpersonal needs theory argues
   a. that relationships have both costs and rewards
   b. electronically mediated communication is different than face-to-face interaction
   c. that the progress of a relationship is based on whether it meets the individual's needs for affection, inclusion and control.
   d. the johari window is flawed

4. In the middle of a conflict situation, you say "All right, you win – I don't want to fight anymore!" This is an example of
   a. withdrawal
   b. forcing
   c. bonding
   d. accommodating

5. The seductiveness of communicating electronically can result in the disruption of ongoing interpersonal relationships. This problem is often due to
   a. dishonesty
   b. technological addiction
   c. anonymity abuse
   d. accommodating

Essay

1. Discuss the five styles of conflict. What are they and when are they appropriate?

2. What are the different strategies that you can use to get information about another? Why is this important for developing relationships?

Useful and Interesting Internet Links

http://www.awc.cc.az.us/psy/dgershaw/lol/Marriages.Last.htm - This site by David Gershaw examines seven reasons why partners think their marriages last.

http://www.etsu.edu/philos/faculty/hugh/honesty.htm - An article from *Journal of Social and Personal Relationships* explores the role of honesty in developing and maintaining personal relationships. By Graham and LaFollette.

http://humanresources.about.com/careers/humanresources/cs/conflictresolves/index.htm?iam=dpile&terms=%2Binterpersonal+%2Bconflict - A long address, but one that leads to a useful site that explores conflict resolution and management. A good review of the distinction between conflict avoidance and conflict prevention.

http://pertinent.com/pertinfo/business/kareCom3.html - "Six Ways to Get Along Better" looks at simple strategies for preventing conflicts.

http://www.geocities.com/research93/ - Close Relationships and Personality Research Web Site has a fun and interesting personality quiz that helps determine your "attachment style."

CHAPTER 9: Interviewing

Learning Objectives
After studying this chapter, you should be able to answer the following questions:
- What should you do to prepare for a job interview?
- What are the important elements of a written resume?
- What are the characteristics of open and closed, primary and secondary, and neutral and leading questions?
- How do you conduct a job interview?
- Can you identify typical questions used by job interviewers?

Interactive Chapter Outline

I. Responsibilities of the Job Applicant

_____

_____

    A. Preparing for the Interview

_____

_____

_____

_____

    B. The Interview

_____

_____

_____

II. Interpersonal Skills in Interviewing Others

_____

_____

A. Determining the Procedure

_____

_____

B. Conducting the Interview

_____

_____

_____

_____

Key Terms

cover letter (p. 220)

_____

_____

resume (p. 221)

_____

_____

interview (p. 229)

_____

_____

open questions (p. 229)

_____

_____

closed questions (p. 230)

_____

_____

neutral questions (p. 230)

_____

_____

leading questions (p. 230)

_____

_____

primary questions (p. 230)

_____

_____

secondary or follow-up questions (p. 230)

_____

_____

Exercises
Journal Activities

📖 Journal Activity 9.1 - Real versus Ideal Resumes (p. 221)
Prepare a draft of your resume based on the skills and accomplishments you have today. Next, draft the ideal resume you wish to have at graduation or five years from now. Then, record your answers to the following questions in the space provided below: (During this exercises, focus on the content of your resume, not the format.)

1. How are the resumes different?

2. What specific actions must you take now to ensure that your future resume looks like your ideal one?

SAMPLE RESUME FORM (Current)

NAME HERE

Address Line 1
Address Line 2
Phone
E-Mail

PROFESSIONAL OBJECTIVE HERE

EDUCATIONAL BACKGROUND HERE

WORK AND OTHER BUSINESS-RELATED EXPERIENCE HERE

PERSONAL INFORMATION HERE

REFERENCES

SAMPLE RESUME FORM (Ideal)

NAME HERE   Address Line 1
                                                   Address Line 2
                                                   Phone
                                                   E-Mail

PROFESSIONAL OBJECTIVE HERE

EDUCATIONAL BACKGROUND HERE

WORK AND OTHER BUSINESS-RELATED EXPERIENCE HERE

PERSONAL INFORMATION HERE

REFERENCES

📖 Journal Activity 9.2 – What Interviewers Look For (p. 230)

Call a large local company and make an appointment to interview a person in the human resources department whose job it is to interview candidates for employment. Develop a set of interview question and follow-ups. Focus your interview on obtaining information about the person's experiences that will help you. For example, you might ask, "What are the characteristics you like to see an interviewee demonstrate?" or "How do you decide whom to interview?" In the space provided below, write the questions you plan to ask, leaving space between each question. During the interview sketch the answers to each of the questions and any follow-up questions you may have used. After you have conducted the interview, be prepared to discuss your findings in class.

Interview Questions and Answers Form:

Company name: _____

Name and title of person interviewed: _____

Date, time and location of interview: _____

Questions and answers:

Journal Activity 9.2 – What Interviewers Look For (cont.)

Interview Questions and Answers Form (cont):

Questions and answers (cont.):

9.3 Using InfoTrac College Edition (p. 222)
Under the subject "cover letter," see "The intelligent standout resume and cover letter," Linda Bates Parker (October, 1998) and "Great letters and why they work," Dean Rieck (June, 1998). Compare their recommendations. Note at least two recommendations on preparing resumes and cover letters that you would want to follow.

9.4 Using InfoTrac College Edition
What skills are required for today's jobs? Using the subject guide, use the search term "job skills." Find the entry for "Comparing 21st century job-skills acquisition with self-fulfillment for college students," E. Scott Ryan (1999). What does the article say are the skills applicants need today? What does the author say about how college students react when they acquire job skills they perceive to be important?

146

9.5 Using Technology (p. 225)

Today many companies post job listings online and allow candidates to complete part of the job search process electronically. Log on to the Internet and go to Monster.com. Look to see whether there are jobs listed in your field. Pay special attention to the application directions. List your results here.

9.6 Using Technology

Many career-oriented web sites like Monster.com not only allow job seekers to browse through job listings, they also offer the ability to post your resume online so that organizations that are seeking applicants may review your qualifications online. Go to one of the career search web sites listed at the end of this chapter and complete the online registration and resume submission process. Some sites allow you to upload a file containing your resume, while others ask you to fill out an online form. Also complete the "career profile" or other online questionnaire used to establish the types of jobs you are seeking or are qualified for. Use your actual list of qualifications and skills, location preference, salary range, etc. Periodically check back to the website and note how many times your resume was viewed and if any potential employers contacted you via e-mail or phone. Be prepared to share your results with the class.

9.7 What Would You Do? (p. 231)
Read the *What Would You Do: A Question of Ethics* scenario on page 231 of your text.
Answer the following questions in the space provided here.

1. Is it interpersonally ethical for Mark to follow Ken's advice? Why?

2. How should we deal with statements like "Everybody does it"?

9.8 Thinking About Perceptions of an Interview (p. 228)
Think of a recent interview you had. Consider the person who interviewed you. How
did your reaction to the interviewer influence your desire to work for that company? Try
to remember what he or she said or did that affected your opinion. Record your notes
below and be prepared to share your thoughts with your class.

9.9 Interview Practice (p. 226 and p. 228)

Using figure 3 on page 226 of your text, enlist a friend to help you practice for an interview. Select a specific job and have your friend interview you using some of the questions listed. After completing the interview, discuss how you performed. Which questions did you handle well, which were hard for you?

9.10 Interview and Resume Review

if you currently have a job, ask your supervisor or the person who interviewed you what influenced their decision to hire you. Focus your questions on the interview and any resume or job application you submitted. Were there specific skills you demonstrated or questions you handled particularly well? Jot down notes based on the responses to your questions and use them as you create an updated resume or prepare for your next job interview.

Chapter 9 Quiz Questions (answers and page references in Appendix)

True/False

1. Despite the proliferation of electronic forms of communication, it is still not possible to locate job opportunities or apply for jobs online.

2. You should plan to arrive 15-20 minutes prior to your appointment for an interview.

3. The job interview is not a place for the job candidate to ask questions of the interviewer.

4. Open questions are broad-based questions designed to allow the interviewee to respond however he or she wishes.

5. Follow-up questions are planned or unplanned questions designed to further pursue the answer to a preceding question.

Multiple Choice

1. Which of the following is not a good thing to do in a cover letter?
   a. include your qualifications
   b. include contact information
   c. address it to "personnel"
   d. keep it short
   e. all of the above are ok.

2. If an interviewer wants an interviewee to express details, ideas and feelings, the interviewer will most likely avoid using
   a. leading questions
   b. open questions
   c. follow-up questions
   d. closed questions

3. Which of the following behaviors is not advised by your text?
   a. starting an extensive conversation about salary and benefits
   b. learning about the company
   c. asking about your specific duties within the company
   d. acting as if you want the job
   e. showing up early for the interview appointment

4. Electronic cover letters and resumes
   a. have become increasingly popular
   b. may be different from paper versions in several ways
   c. usually should be kept simple in format

      d. can be posted on a personal home page
      e. all of the above

5. According to a recent survey,
      a. online resumes are not useful
      b. company research is usually useless in an interview situation
      c. personal appearance is the leading factor in candidate rejection
      d. answering questions without any hesitation is better than taking some time to think about your answer.

Essay

1. Discuss the three different types of questions and their purposes that interviewers ask.

2. What are the key points of information that should be included in a resume?

Useful and Interesting Internet Links

http://www.monster.com - A free site for posting your resume and looking for jobs. You can search by location, job type, etc.

http://www.employment911.com - similar to Monster.com, employment911 claims to have over three million job listings.

http://www.123-jobs.com/job-interview-questions.shtml - 123-jobs.com has a page devoted to interview tips and techniques.

http://jobsearch.about.com/careers/jobsearch/cs/interviews/index.htm - This site from About.com offers a long list of interview resources including a long list of questions commonly asked by interviewers and a long list of questions interviewees should consider asking.

http://www.vscc.cc.tn.us/academic/humanities/comm/careers.htm - This site offers a long list of career resources for communication majors, but it is also useful for job seekers from other fields as well. A good list of links.

III

GROUP COMMUNICATION

CHAPTER 10: Participating in Group Communication

Learning Objectives
After studying this chapter, you should be able to answer the following questions:
- What characterizes effective groups?
- How can group discussion lead to improving group goal statements?
- What is the optimum size for a group?
- What factors affect cohesiveness in groups?
- How can a group improve its cohesiveness?
- How do groups form, maintain, and change their norms?
- How does the physical setting affect group interaction?
- What are the stages of group development?
- What are the steps of the problem-solving method?
- What constraints result in groups being ineffective at problem-solving, and how can they be managed?

Interactive Chapter Outline

I. Characteristics of Effective Work Groups

_____

_____

    A. Developing Clearly Defined Goals to which Members are Committed

_____

_____

    B. Optimum Number of Diverse Members

_____

_____

    C. Cohesiveness

_____

_____

D. Norms

_____

_____

E. Physical Setting

_____

_____

II. Stages of Group Development

_____

_____

A. Forming

_____

_____

B. Storming

_____

_____

C. Norming

_____

_____

D. Performing

_____

_____

E. Adjourning

_____

_____

III. Problem Solving in Groups

_____

_____

A. Defining the Problem

_____

_____

B. Analyzing the Problem

_____

_____

C. Determining Solution Criteria

_____

_____

D. Identifying Possible Solutions

_____

_____

E. Evaluating Solutions

_____

_____

F. Deciding

_____

_____

_____

_____

IV. Constraints on Effective Decision Making

_____

_____

Key Terms

work group (p. 238)

_____

_____

group goal (p. 238)

_____

_____

specific goal (p. 239)

_____

_____

consistent goals (p. 239)

_____

_____

challenging goals (p. 239)

_____

_____

acceptable goals (p. 239)

_____

_____

homogenous group (p. 240)

_____

_____

heterogeneous group (p. 240)

_____

156

cohesiveness (p. 240)

team building activities (p. 242)

norms (p. 243)

ground rules (p. 243)

working environment (p. 244)

forming (p. 246)

storming (p. 247)

groupthink (p. 247)

norming (p. 248)

performing (p. 248)

_____

_____

adjourning (p. 248)

_____

_____

questions of fact (p. 251)

_____

_____

questions of value (p. 251)

_____

_____

questions of policy (p. 251)

_____

_____

brainstorming (p. 253)

_____

_____

decision making (p. 255)

_____

_____

cognitive constraints (p. 258)

_____

_____

affiliative constraints (p. 258)

_____

_____

158

devil's advocate (p. 259)

_____

_____

egocentric constraints (p. 259)

_____

_____

Exercises
Journal Activities

📖 Journal Activity 10.1 – Board Member Skills (p. 240)
Visit the web site of a large company, such as General Motors, General Electric, or Coca Cola. Search the site and find the names and brief background sketches of the members of the Board of Directors. Analyze the ways in which the members are similar or different. Answer the following questions in the space provided below:

1. What relevant knowledge and skills might each bring to the group's decision process?

2. What viewpoints are not represented by the board members?

3. How might an absence of these viewpoints affect their discussions?

Journal Activity 10.2 – Physical Settings (p. 246)

During the next week, keep a record of all the group settings you participate in. Note the physical setting (location, temperature, size of space, seating configuration), the interaction patterns (who talks, who listens, who agrees, who disagrees), and your satisfaction with the group discussion (high to low). At the end of the week, analyze these data to see how the physical settings might have influenced group interaction and your satisfaction with the process. What conclusions can you draw?

Physical Setting:

Interaction Patterns:

Satisfaction:

Analysis:

📖 Journal Activity 10.3 – Decision Methods (p. 256)

Remember an instance where a group you were part of made a poor decision using a majority-rule method. In the space provided below, analyze why the decision was a poor one. Answer the following questions: Would a different decision method have helped? If so, what method might have been more effective? Why?

<u>10.4 Using InfoTrac College Edition (p. 255)</u>
Under the subject "problem solving discussion," click on "periodical references." Scroll to "group problem solving." Since teamwork is a "hot topic," see "teamworking in its contexts: Antecedents, nature and dimensions." Look for information on different designs for teams. Summarize your findings here.

<u>10.5 Using InfoTrac College Edition</u>
How can we improve our ability to brainstorm effectively? Under the subject "problem solving discussion," click on "periodical references." Scroll to "group problem solving." Find the article "Some Brainstorming Exercises," by Ethan M. Rasiel. (*Across the Board*, June 2000.) Summarize the article's techniques here.

10.6 Using InfoTrac College Edition

Type in the key words "effective group work" and locate the article titled "How to get a group to perform like a team," by Blanchard, Carew and Parsi-Carew. Do you think the PERFORM method would work in a classroom?

10.7 Using the Web – Groupthink (p. 247)

For a complete discussion of groupthink, see Shannon's Group Think Application at http://oak.cats.ohiou.edu/~sk260695/skthink.html What are the causes of groupthink? What can members of a group do to avoid groupthink in their decision-making process?

10.8 Using the Web

Using one of the Internet search engines, enter the search phrase "small group communication." Count the number of links the search engine returns. Browse through the links presented and select one that is educational in nature. (You may find course syllabi, instructional sites, information resources, and the like.) Review the content of the site and any relevant links provided therein. Summarize your findings below. Compare the information you found with that in the text. Are there any differences?

<u>10.9 What Would You Do? (p. 259)</u>
Read the *What Would You Do: A Question of Ethics* scenario on page 259 of your text. Answer the following questions in the space provided here.

1. What did the group really know about the Boardman Center? Is it good group discussion practice to rely on a passing comment on one member?

2. Regardless of whether the meeting went smoothly, is there any ethical problem with this process? Explain.

10.10 Thinking About Group Goals (p. 239)

Have you ever participated in a study group? Did the group discuss its goals? What affect did presence of or failure of discussing group goals have on the outcome?

10.11 Thinking About Cohesiveness (p. 242)

Can a high level of cohesiveness in a group actually become counterproductive? Have you ever been a part of such a group? If so, consider how high cohesiveness hurt the group's decision-making ability. Write your answers below and be prepared to share your thoughts with the class.

Chapter 10 Quiz Questions (answers and page references in Appendix)

True/False

1. Effective groups are most likely to be made up of heterogeneous members.

2. The consensus method for group decision-making is the same thing as a unanimous decision.

3. The expert opinion method for deciding puts final responsibility for a decision in the hands of the group member with the greatest knowledge or expertise in the matter.

4. Physical location and setting have little impact on the workings of a group.

5. "A collection of three or more people who must interact and influence one another to accomplish a common purpose" is the definition of a "cohesive group."

Multiple Choice

1. The process of choosing among alternatives is
    a. decision making
    b. norming
    c. performing
    d. storming

2. "What should we do to reduce air pollution?" is an example of what type of question?
    a. question of fact
    b. question of policy
    c. question of value
    d. question of norming
    e. question of skill

3. Tammy shows up late for a group meeting. The discussion had already begun and as she entered the room, she was greeted by several angry looks. Which of the following best explains their reaction to Tammy's tardiness?
    a. storming was in progress
    b. norms had not yet been established
    c. groupthink was occurring
    d. an on-time norm had been developed by that group

4. Adjourning is
    a. the end of group meetings
    b. the stage of group development where members assign meaning to what they have done
    c. the stage of group development concerned with the establishment of group

standards
d. none of the above

5. A group decides to define the problem it has been tasked to decide as follows: "Should the company abolish the current pension plan and abolish the current dental plan." This group has committed which error in problem consideration:
   a. The problem should use specific and precise language.
   b. The problem should be stated as a question.
   c. The problem should be a policy issue.
   d. The problem should contain only one central idea.
   e. The group has committee no error.

Essay

1. Discuss the three different types of questions. How are each type identified?

2. What are the characteristics of an ideal group goal? Why are such goals important to the effective functioning of a work group?

Useful and Interesting Internet Links

http://www.gm.com - The web address for General Motors, Inc.

http://www.generalelectric.com - The web address for General Electric, Inc.

http://www.coke.com - The web address for The Coca Cola Company.

http://www.brocku.ca/commstudies/courses/2F50/effective.html - A list of factors that influence effective group communication from Brock University's Communication Studies program.

http://sociology.about.com/science/sociology/cs/groupthink/index.htm - About.com's page on the concept of groupthink. A thorough review.

http://www.bethany.edu/psych/psychbib/tnk/decision.txt - A bibliography of texts on decision-making.

CHAPTER 11: Member Roles and Leadership in Groups

Learning Objectives

After studying this chapter, you should be able to answer the following questions:

- What are roles, and why are they important in groups?
- How do members choose their roles?
- What types of roles do members of groups enact?
- What behaviors are expected of all members to make group meetings effective?
- What is leadership and why is it important to a group?
- What are the tasks of leadership?
- What characterizes the communication behavior of leaders?
- How does leadership develop in a group?
- What behaviors can help an individual become a leader?
- What should the leader of a meeting do to make the meeting successful?

Interactive Chapter Outline

I. Member Roles

_____

_____

   A. Task-oriented Roles

_____

_____

   B. Maintenance Roles

_____

_____

   C. Procedural Roles

_____

_____

D. Self-Centered Roles

_____

_____

E. Normal Distribution of Roles

_____

_____

II. Member Responsibilities in Group Meetings

_____

_____

A. Preparing for the Meeting

_____

_____

B. Participating in the Meeting

_____

_____

C. Following-up the Meeting

_____

_____

III. Leadership

_____

_____

A. The Function of Leadership

_____

_____

170

B. Types of Leaders

_____

_____

C. How Members Gain and Maintain Informal Leadership

_____

_____

D. Gender Differences in Emerging Leaders

_____

_____

IV. Leading Group Meetings

_____

_____

A. Before the Meeting

_____

_____

B. During the Meeting

_____

_____

_____

_____

C. Meeting Follow-up

_____

_____

V. Evaluating Group Effectiveness

_____

_____

A. The Decision

_____

_____

B. Individual Participation and Role Behavior

_____

_____

_____

_____

C. Leadership

_____

_____

Key Terms

role (p. 264)

_____

_____

task-related role (p. 264)

_____

_____

information or opinion giver (p. 264)

_____

_____

information or opinion seeker (p. 264)

_____

172

analyzer (p. 264)

maintenance role (p. 265)

supporters (p. 265)

tension reliever (p. 265)

harmonizer (p. 265)

interpreters (p. 265)

procedural role (p. 266)

expediter (p. 266)

recorder (p. 266)

minutes (p. 266)

gatekeeper (p. 266)

self-centered role (p. 267)

aggressor (p. 267)

joker (p. 276)

withdrawer (p. 276)

monopolizer (p. 267)

leadership (p. 271)

informal leaders (p. 272)

framing (p. 273)

_____

_____

Exercises
Journal Activities

Journal Activity 11.1 – Preparing an Analysis Grid (p. 268)
Using the page provided below, prepare an analysis grid listing each of the roles
discussed in Chapter 11 of your text as rows and listing spaces for each of the
participants as columns. Find a group you want to use to practice recording data. Put a
check mark in the appropriate row and column each time you see a particular member
enacting a behavior associated with a specific role. For example, if Maria responds to a
comment by another member by saying "good observation," then you would record a
check under her name in the row "supporter." Review the data to determine all positive
and negative roles performed. Then, answer this question: What is the value of this
kind of data collection to a person advising a group about their interactions?

Answer question here:

📖 Journal Activity 11.1 – Preparing an Analysis Grid (Sample Analysis Grid)

Names of Participants

ROLE:					
Info/Opinion Giver					
Info/Opinion Seeker					
Analyzers					
Supporters					
Tension Relievers					
Harmonizers					
Interpreters					
Expediters					
Recorders					
Gatekeepers					
Aggressors					
Jokers					
Withdrawers					
Monopolizers					

Notes:

Journal Activity 11.2 – Emerging Roles and Leadership (p. 272)

Identify a recently formed group of at least five members to which you belong where informal leaders have emerged. In the space provided below, identify the roles that each member of the group seems to play. Remember, a member may perform more than one role. Then answer the following questions: Is there a formal leader? Who are the informal leaders? How did they emerge? What is it that each does that leads you to believe that person is fulfilling leadership functions? Why was each of the other members of the group eliminated from informal leadership? Suppose the goal of your group was changed. In what way might this affect the leadership of the group?

Member:	Roles:

<u>11.3 Using InfoTrac College Edition (p. 271)</u>
Under the subject "leadership," click on "periodical references." Scroll to "Principles of Leadership," by Edward Moyers, July 15, 2000. Look for the heading "II: Leadership is not a popularity contest," and find the statement "Respect is what a true leader strives for – not just to be liked by all the people you are involved with." Of the eight ways of earning respect, which one or two do you believe it is most important to put into practice? Why?

<u>11.4 Using InfoTrac College Edition</u>
What does it take to be an effective leader? Under the subject "leadership," click on "periodical references." Scroll to "Lead, follow, or get out of the way," by Marcia A. Reed-Woodard, April 2001. What does the author say about the importance of knowing the people you are leading? Summarize the article below.

11.5 Using Technology

Using the link to the listing of college and university programs in leadership provided in the Useful and Interesting Internet Links section of this chapter, select several school programs and visit each one. Note the course listings and descriptions provided. Note also any special projects, internships or experiential learning requirements the programs might have. Summarize your findings below and be prepared to share your information with your classmates. Why do you suppose these courses and activities are required?

<u>11.6 What Would You Do? (p. 283)</u>
Read the *What Would You Do: A Question of Ethics* scenario on page 283 of your text. Answer the following questions in the space provided here.

1. Should Sue follow Heather's advice? Why or Why not?

2. What would you do if you were in Heather's situation? What advice would you give Sue?

<u>11.7 Thinking about Roles (p. 266)</u>
Which of the three roles (task, maintenance, procedural) discussed in the Member Roles section of Chapter 11 do you perform the most frequently when you are in a group? Which role is easiest for you to perform? Which role is most difficult for you? Why?

11.8 Thinking About Member Responsibilities (p. 270)

Consider your own behavior when you are a member of a group. Which of the preparation, participation, and follow-up guidelines do you need to work on to become a more valuable member of a problem-solving group? Why?

11.9 Evaluating Group Decisions

How effective are groups when they need to make decisions? Using the sample form for evaluating group decisions found on the next page, analyze how effective a group you belong to is when making decisions. You may wish to use the same groups analyzed for exercises 11.1 and 11.2. Based on your analysis, how effective was the group? What could the group do to become more effective in decision making?

Answer questions here:

11.9, cont. **Group Decision Making Evaluation Form**

(Rate the group as a whole on each of the following questions using this scale: 1 = never, 2 = rarely, 3 = sometimes, 4 = often, 5 = always.)

Group Characteristics:

_____ 1. Did the group have a clearly defined goal to which most members were committed?

_____ 2. Did the group's size fit the tasks required to meet its goals?

_____ 3. Was group member diversity sufficient to ensure that important viewpoints were expressed?

_____ 4. Did group cohesiveness aid in task accomplishment?

_____ 5. Did group norms help accomplish goals and maintain relationships?

_____ 6. Was the physical setting conducive to accomplishing the work?

Member Relationships:

_____ 1. Did members feel valued and respected by others?

_____ 2. Were members comfortable interacting with others?

_____ 3. Did members balance speaking time so that all members participated?

_____ 4. Were conflicts seen as positive experiences?

_____ 5. Did members like and enjoy each other?

Group Problem Solving:

_____ 1. Did the group take time to define its problem?

_____ 2. Was high-quality information presented to help the group understand the problem?

_____ 3. Did the group develop criteria before suggesting solutions?

_____ 4. Were the criteria discussed sufficiently and based on all the information available?

_____ 5. Did the group use effective brainstorming techniques to develop a comprehensive list of creative alternative solutions?

_____ 6. Did the group fairly and thoroughly compare each alternative to all solution criteria?

_____ 7. Did the group follow its decision rules in choosing among alternatives that had met the criteria?

_____ 8. Did the group arrive at a decision that members agreed to support?

11.10 Evaluating Individual Participation in Groups

The behavior of individuals within a group is important to the overall success of the group. The form that follows provides a method toe valuate the contributions of individuals to the group process. Use the form to critique one member of the group that was analyzed in exercise 11.9. Then write an analysis of that individual's participation in the space provided below.

Analysis of Group Member:

11.10, cont. Individual Participation Evaluation Form

(Rate the participant named on each of the following categories using this scale: 1 = never, 2 = rarely, 3 = sometimes, 4 = often, 5 = always.)

Meeting Behavior:

_____ 1. Prepared and knowledgeable

_____ 2. Contributed ideas and opinions

_____ 3. Actively listened to the ideas of others

_____ 4. Politely voiced disagreement

_____ 5. Completed between meetings assigned tasks

Performance of Task-Oriented Roles:

_____ 1. Acted as information or opinion giver

_____ 2. Acted as information seeker

_____ 3. Acted as Analyzer

Performance of Procedural Roles:

_____ 1. Acted as expediter

_____ 2. Acted as recorder

_____ 3. Acted as gatekeeper

Performance of Maintenance Roles:

_____ 1. Acted as Supporter

_____ 2. Acted as Tension Reliever

_____ 3. Acted as Harmonizer

_____ 4. Acted as Interpreter

Avoided Self-Centered Roles:

_____ 1. Avoided acting as Aggressor

_____ 2. Avoided acting as Joker

_____ 3. Avoided acting as Withdrawer

_____ 4. Avoided acting as Monopolizer

Chapter 11 Quiz Questions (answers and page references in Appendix)

True/False

1. An Analysis Grid is a tool used to track which group members enact behavior associated with group roles.

2. Approximately 15% of group time should be devoted to information sharing.

3. A member may perform only one role in a group.

4. It is usually not a good idea for leaders to speak to group members before a group meeting as it may influence how the members communicate with the leader in the meeting.

5. It is possible for a group to have more than one leader.

Multiple Choice

1. Which of the following is *not* one of the four types of roles discussed in the text?
   a. task-oriented
   b. maintenance
   c. procedural
   d. other-centered
   e. self-centered

2. In a problem-solving group, Narika provides the group with data that helps it to make an effective decision. Narika's role can be described as
   a. information or opinion giver
   b. information or opinion seeker
   c. analyzer
   d. harmonizer

3. Carlos notices the group is in a lethargic, tense state. He tells a quick joke to get everyone to lighten up. Carlos is trying to be an effective
   a. interpreter
   b. harmonizer
   c. tension reliever
   d. maintainer
   e. expediter

4. Len has been appointed the chair of the committee in charge of selecting a new student representative to the governing board. He is what type of leader?
   a. informal
   b. formal

    c. charismatic
    d. framing

5. The process of influencing members to accomplish group goals is the definition of
    a. roles
    b. leadership
    c. maintenance
    d. framing

Essay

1. Discuss the differences between formal and informal leadership. Note differences in the areas of how one becomes a leader and how one maintains leadership.

2. What are some of the guidelines the text provides to assist leaders in making meetings more productive? Of all of these, which do you feel is the most important and why?

Useful and interesting Internet Links

http://ww4.choice.net/~marybast/ldrho.htm - This site describes none leadership styles and offers advice for the development of skills aimed at reducing problems associated with each style. By Mary R. Bast.

http://www.looksmart.com/eus1/eus317829/eus317861/eus578394/eus280516/eus2796 99/r?l& - A long address, but it leads to a thorough listing of college and university programs in organizational leadership. Some of the links provided lead directly to extensive online leadership resources.

http://www.squarewheel.com - A humorous look at leadership, teamwork and related issues.

http://www.wcer.wise.edu/nise/cl1/CL/doingcl/grproles.htm - This site focuses on group roles and collaboration within groups.

http://www.ncrel.org/ncrel/sdrs/areas/issues/content/cntareas/science/eric/eric7.htm - This site is devoted to student work groups.

IV

PUBLIC SPEAKING

CHAPTER 12: Determining Your Goal

Learning Objectives

After studying this chapter, you should be able to answer the following questions:

- How do you brainstorm for topics?
- How do you compile audience data?
- How do you predict the level of interest in, knowledge of, and attitude toward a topic?
- What are the key physical and psychological conditions affecting the speech?
- How do you test your speech goal?

Interactive Chapter Outline

I. Selecting a Topic from a Subject Area

_____

_____

A. Identifying Subjects

_____

_____

B. Brainstorming for Topics

_____

_____

II. Analyzing the Audience

_____

_____

A. Kinds of Audience Data Needed

_____

_____

B. Ways of Gathering Data

_____

_____

C. Using Data to Predict Audience Reactions

_____

_____

III. Considering the Setting

_____

_____

_____

_____

_____

_____

_____

IV. Writing the Speech Goal

_____

_____

A. General Goal

_____

_____

B. Specific Goal

_____

_____

_____

_____

C. Relationship Among Subjects, Topics, Goals and Thesis Statements

_____

_____

Key Terms

subject (p. 290)

_____

_____

topic (p. 290)

_____

_____

brainstorming (p. 291)

_____

_____

audience analysis (p. 293)

_____

_____

credibility (p. 296)

_____

_____

setting (p. 296)

_____

_____

general goal (p. 298)

_____

_____

190

specific goal (p. 299)

_____

_____

thesis statement (p. 301)

_____

_____

Exercises
Journal Activities

📖 Journal Activity 12.1 – Brainstorming for Topics (p. 292)

Fill in the three columns below with at least twenty related topics for each column. Check one topic in each column that has special meaning to you or that seems particularly appropriate for your classroom audience. Then select one topic from these three of your first speech.

Major or Vocational Interest	Hobby or Activity	Issue or Concern

📖 Journal Activity 12.2 – Analyzing Your Audience (p. 295)

Complete the audience analysis checklist shown below.

1. Next to the second heading, Predictions, write the topic you plan to use for your first speech.

2. Fill in the checklist, including both data about your classroom audience and predictions about their reactions to your topic.

3. Save the results. You will use the data from this checklist to help you determine a strategy for adapting to your audience.

Checklist: Audience Analysis

Data

1. The audience education level is _____ high school _____ college _____ post-college.

2. The age range is from _____ to _____. The average age is about _____.

3. The audience is approximately _____ percent male and _____ percent female.

4. My estimate of the average income level of the audience is _____ below average _____ average _____ above average.

5. The audience is basically _____ the same race _____ a mixture of races.

6. The audience is basically _____ the same religion _____ a mixture of religions.

7. The audience is basically _____ the same nationality _____ a mixture of nationalities.

8. The audience is basically from _____ the same state _____ the same city _____ the same neighborhood _____ different areas.

Predictions (Topic: _____)

1. Audience interest in this topic is likely to be _____ high _____ moderate _____ low, because _____.

2. Audience understanding of the topic will be _____ great _____ moderate _____ little, because _____.

3. Audience attitude toward me as a speaker is likely to be _____ positive _____ neutral _____ negative, because _____.

4. Audience attitude toward my topic will be _____ positive _____ neutral _____ negative, because _____.

Journal Activity 12.3 – Analyzing the Occasion and Setting (p. 298)

Complete the Occasion and Setting Checklist below.

1. Answer the questions about the occasion and setting for your first speech.
2. Save the results. You will use the data from this checklist to help you determine strategies for adapting to your audience.

Checklist: Occasion and Setting

1. Where will the speech be given?

2. How large will the audience be?

3. When will the speech be given?

4. Where in the program does the speech occur?

5. What is the time limit for the speech?

6. What are the expectations for the speech?

7. What equipment is necessary to give the speech?

Journal Activity 12.4 – Writing Speech Goals (p. 301)

In the space provided below, follow the five-step procedure outlined in your text, write a speech goal for the topic you have selected for your first speech. Save your work.

1. Write a first draft of your goal that includes the infinitive phrase that articulates the response you want from your audience.

2. Revise your first draft until you have written a complete sentence that specifies the nature of the audience response.

3. Make sure the goal only contains one idea.

4. Revise the infinitive or the infinitive phrase until it indicates the specific audience reaction desired.

5. Write at least three versions of the goal. Pick the clearest goal or the one whose emphasis is most to your liking.

12.5 Using InfoTrac College Edition (p. 300)
Access InfoTrac College Edition and click on PowerTrac. From the search index, choose Journal name (jn). Press on Key Word and drag down to Journal name. Enter "Vital Speeches." View Vital Speeches and find a speech on a topic that interests you. Then read that speech and identify the speaker's goal. Was the goal clearly stated in the introduction? Was it implied but clear? Was it unclear? Note how this analysis can help you clarify your own speech goal.

12.6 Using InfoTrac College Edition
Using the same InfoTrac College Edition PowerTrac search as in exercise 12.5, select a speech on a topic that at first glance does not seem interesting to you, but that you think may be relevant to you in some way. Read that speech. When you are done, answer the following questions in the space provided below: After reading the speech, did you find it more interesting than you originally thought? Why? What did the speaker do to try and draw you into the topic, or make the topic seem more interesting or relevant than you originally thought it would be? Note how this analysis can help you as you prepare your own speeches.

12.7 Using Technology - Attitude Toward Your Topic (p. 295)
There are many organizations that poll public opinion on topics. If you have no idea about how your specific audience might react to your topic, you may be able to find some idea of general attitudes by accessing public opinion polls. The following web sites are good places to look for opinion polls:
http://www.WashingtonPost.com (Click on "Politics," then Polls.")
http://www.pollingreport.com
http://www.gallup.com
Visit each of these sites and examine the polling data available. These may be useful for your speeches.

12.8 What Would You Do? (p. 303)
Read the *What Would You Do: A Question of Ethics* scenario on page 303 of your text. Answer the following questions in the space provided here.

1. What is the ethical issue at stake?

2. Was there anything about Glen's behavior that was unethical? Anything about Adam's?

3. What should be the penalty, if any, for Glen? For Adam?

12.9 Relationship Among Subject, Topic, Goal and Thesis Statement

Using information about your first speech and the results of exercises 12.1, 12.4, and 12.5, complete the following worksheet. Save your work, as it will be important for the development of your speech. (See examples on page 302 of your text. Thesis statements are discussed further in Ch. 14.))

Subject Area:

Topic:

General Speech Goal:

Specific Goal:

Thesis Statement:

12.10 From the Audience's Perspective

Using the form from exercise 12.2 and a partner, analyze a speech topic from the perspective of the audience. Have a partner from your class provide you with his/her speech topic, goals and thesis statement. As an audience member, how would you react to this speech? Fill out the "Predictions" portion of the form found in 12.2 accordingly. Your partner will be doing the same for your speech. After both of you have completed the forms, exchange them. How is the form you filled out in 12.2 different from the one your partner filled out? If there are differences, how might they affect the preparation of your speech?

Chapter 12 Quiz Questions (answers and page references in Appendix)

True/False

1. Thesis statements and goal statements are the same.

2. "A broad area of knowledge" is the definition of a topic.

3. Personal observation can be a useful method of gathering data about an audience.

4. You will be less likely to be able to move about when the audience is much larger than approximately 50 people.

5. Most speeches can be classified as speeches that are meant to persuade, inform or entertain.

Multiple Choice

1. The method for generating topics discussed in the text is called
    a. brainstorming
    b. analyzing
    c. adapting
    d. recording

2. The sentence: "I want the audience to understand the procedure for registering for classes at the college" is an example of
    a. general speech goal
    b. thesis statement
    c. specific goal
    d. topic sentence
    e. none of the above

3. The size of the audience
    a. has no bearing on speech preparation
    b. may limit how much you are able to move around
    c. may require you to wear a microphone
    d. b and c

4. Tiffany is sitting in the class she will be giving a speech to in the future. She looks around the room, noting the average age of her classmates, their gender and ethnic makeup. Tiffany is engaging in what practice?
    a. group affiliation
    b. uniqueness
    c. brainstorming
    d. data gathering by observation

5. Antwon is analyzing his audience. Which of the following should he not consider when doing this?

>   a. audience attitude toward the speaker
>   b. audience attitude toward the setting
>   c. audience attitude toward the topic
>   d. audience interest in the topic
>   e. all are discussed in the text as important to consider

Essay

1. Define and discuss audience analysis. Focus on why it is it important to know about your audience before you give a speech.

2. Why is it important to have a clear speech goal? Discuss this from the perspective of both audience and speaker.

Useful and Interesting Internet Links

http://www.public-speaking.org/public-speaking-articles.htm#topic - A series of articles on topic development from the Advanced Public Speaking Institute

http://www.public-speaking.org/public-speaking-articles.htm - A few articles on the audience.

http://www.toastmasters.org/ - The homepage for Toastmaster's International, an organization devoted to improving speaking skills.

http://www.ukans.edu/cwis/units/coms2/vpa/vpa2.htm - Another site devoted to topic selection, this page is part of the University of Kansas' Virtual Presentation Assistant.

http://www.ukans.edu/cwis/units/coms2/vpa/vpa1.htm - The University of Kansas' Virtual Presentation Assistant provides help with determining the purpose of your speech.

http://www.pollingreport.com - Contains lists of public polling results.

http://www.gallup.com - Gallup is an organization devoted to research on public opinion. Much polling data can be found here.

CHAPTER 13: Research

Learning Objectives
After studying this chapter, you should be able to answer the following questions:
- What are the key sources of information for speeches?
- What is the difference between factual and opinion statements?
- How can you determine whether a source will be useful?
- What should be included on note cards?
- What is the best way to cite sources in a speech?

Interactive Chapter Outline

I. Where to Look: Traditional and Electronic Sources of Information

_____

_____

A. Personal Knowledge, Experience, and Observation

_____

_____

B. Library Manual and Electronic Research

_____

_____

_____

_____

C. The Internet

_____

_____

D. Tips for Researching

_____

_____

E. Skimming to Determine Source Value

_____

_____

F. Interviewing

_____

_____

G. Surveys

_____

_____

II. What Information to Look For

_____

_____

A. Factual Statements

_____

_____

B. Expert Opinion

_____

_____

C. Verbal forms of Information

_____

_____

III. Recording Data and Citing Electronic and Written Sources

_____

_____

  A. Recording Data

_____

_____

  B. Citing Sources in Speeches

_____

_____

_____

_____

Key Terms

electronic database (p. 309)

_____

_____

periodicals (p. 311)

_____

_____

Internet (p. 313)

_____

_____

skimming (p. 314)

_____

_____

interviewing (p. 315)

_____

202

open questions (p. 316)

closed questions (p. 316)

leading questions (p. 316)

neutral questions (p. 316)

follow-up questions (p. 316)

survey (p. 317)

factual statements (p. 319)

expert opinions (p. 319)

examples (p. 322)

hypothetical examples (p. 322)

statistics (p. 322)

anecdotes (p. 324)

narratives (p. 324)

comparisons (p. 324)

contrasts (p. 325)

plagiarism (p. 326)

Exercises
Journal Activities

Journal Activity 13.1 – Listing Sources (p. 318)
For the topic you selected for your first speech, fill in the following information in the spaces provided on the next page.

📖 Journal Activity 13.1 – Listing Sources (cont.)

1. Working with manual or computerized versions of your library's card catalog or periodical indexes (including InfoTrac College Edition), list a total of six books and/or magazine articles that appear to provide information for your topic.

2. Name a person you could interview for additional information for this topic.

3. Write survey questions – if a survey is appropriate.

13.2 Using InfoTrac College Edition (p. 313)

Use InfoTrac College Edition to find information on the subject you have selected for your speech. Click on periodical references. Look for articles that include information that seems relevant to your speech. Whether you download the article or make note cards, make sure that you have the necessary data to cite the source of information if you use it in your speech.

13.3 Using InfoTrac College Edition

Sometimes a search on your subject area may turn up few or no periodical references, or those that are returned do not contain information relevant to your specific purpose. What can be done in that case? Often times, a modified search may be more fruitful. Using InfoTrac College Edition, try modifying your search terms. For example, if you originally entered "decision making in small group communication," you may not have turned up many references. But if you entered "decision making" or "group communication," you will return many more periodical references. Try several different words and phrases related to your topic to return the most comprehensive list of results. Skim the articles that seem most relevant and save those that may be of use to you.

13.4 Using Technology (p. 314)

Online indexes and databases available through libraries as well as the Internet can be used to find sources for supporting material for your speeches. Check with your college or public library to see what indexes and databases you can access through them. For instance, using the Internet, you can access *The Statistical Abstract of the United States* at http://www.census.gov. As practice, visit the site and key in "U.S., crime, statistics." Spend a few minutes acquainting yourself with this site. How might you use this information in a speech on mandatory sentencing?

13.5 Using Technology – Library Orientation

Most college and university libraries maintain access to several electronic databases in addition to Internet access. In many cases, such as at small schools or community colleges, electronic databases may be the most robust sources of timely information available. In any cases, you will likely employ these resources to some extent. Call or drop by your circulation and reference desk to make an appointment with a librarian in order to receive an overview of what resources are available and instructions on their use. Many libraries have printed instructions as well and Internet-based tutorials as well. Practice using the resources available. Your research will be more efficient if you are knowledgeable in the use of various electronic databases. (Some libraries offer access to their electronic databases through their web pages as well.)

13.6 Using the Web

The Internet can be a valuable source of information for your speeches. Using one of the search engines listed in the "Useful and Interesting Internet Links" section of this chapter, search for information on the topic of your speech. Skim through the most promising results and write down or download full citation information. List all the sources that may be useful in the space below.

13.7 Using the Web

Search engines are not the only useful sources of information on the Internet. Most large media outlets and other sources of news and information have a presence on the Internet. Using the links provided in the "Useful and Interesting Internet Links" section of this chapter, search some media and reference resources for information on your topic. You may find further links, full text of articles and/or visual information such as graphics, photos or video. Take full notes, download or print any relevant information you find. Be sure to compile full bibliographic information for citing your sources.

13.8 Test Your Competence (p. 329)

Using information from books, magazines, journals, newspapers, or online sources that you found in Exercises 13.1, 13.2, 13.3, 13.5, and 13.6, prepare note cards citing information such as examples and illustrations, statistics, anecdotes and narratives, comparisons and contrasts, quotations, definitions, or descriptions that you can consider using for your first speech.

On your note cards, be sure to include the publication data for the books, magazines, journals, newspapers, or online sources. (See pages 326-328 in your text for what information to compile.)

Save your note cards.

13.9 What Would You Do? (p. 329)

Read the *What Would You Do: A Question of Ethics* scenario on page 329 of your text. Answer the following questions in the space provided here.

1. What do you think of Tom's assessment of his use of statistics that "No one is going to say anything about it"?

2. Does Tom have any further ethical obligation? If so, what is it?

13.10 Quotations

Locate a book of quotations. *Bartlett's Familiar Quotations* is a popular example found in most libraries. Internet sites with similar information also exist. Skim through the book or browse the web site. Seek quotes relevant to your speech and write a few in the space below. How may these be used to enhance your speech? If quotations directly relevant to your topic are not found, how may a quote still be useful? What can it add to a speech? (Be sure to copy full bibliographic information concerning the source of the quote.)

Chapter 13 Quiz Questions (answers and page references in Appendix)

True/False

1. Since note cards can be easily misplaced, they should not be used in speech research.

2. A variety of information from diverse sources is preferable when researching a speech.

3. In order to not mislead your audience, us statistics that are both recent and older.

4. "Skimming" references should never be done as you can miss crucial details.

5. Personal knowledge and experience may be useful in a speech.

Multiple Choice

1. Personal knowledge and experience
    a. are not valid sources of information for prepared speeches
    b. can be supplemented by careful observation
    c. can be useful if your topic is something you know about
    d. b and c
    e. none of the above

2. Which of these is not mentioned as a source for information for your speeches?
    a. personal experience
    b. library research
    c. your instructor
    d. electronic databases

3. If your topic is "in the news", which of the following is likely true:
    a. books will be better sources since they offer depth of information
    b. electronic databases will not be good sources as they are not kept current
    c. encyclopedias will likely be your only source of information
    d. periodicals will likely be your primary source of information as they are more current than books.

4. Interviews
    a. are not useful sources for speeches
    b. are best left to professionals
    c. can be very effective if you ask the right person good questions
    d. are great to use because they require no preparation

5. Expert opinions
   a. are judgments and interpretations made by authorities in a particular subject area.
   b. do not carry weight with any audiences
   c. can take the place of facts entirely
   d. are often more useful than facts
   e. can only be used in subject areas where there are no facts

Essay

1. Discuss what information should be placed on note cards? Why should note cards be used instead of a sheet or sheets of paper?

2. Why is it often important to draw sources from a variety of backgrounds?

Useful and Interesting Internet Links

http://www.census.gov - This site compiles statistical data on the population of the United States. Much of it is derived from the most current census. Very useful for gathering statistical data on a wide range of topics.

http://www.yahoo.com - A popular web search engine.

http://www.dogpile.com - Another search engine. Dogpile works by searching a list of other search engines and then presents the results in search engine order.

http://www.nytimes.com - The website for *The New York Times*. An excellent source for current information on national and world news. *The New York Times* is generally considered a "newspaper of record."

http://www.cnn.com - The website for Cable News Network, the 24 hour news cable television network. CNN presents a wide variety of national and international news, sports, weather and features and includes an archive of older material and links to related websites.

http://www.ukans.edu/cwis/units/coms2/vpa/vpa3.htm - This link accesses research resources for speech writing provided by the University of Kansas' *Virtual Presentation Assistant*.

http://www.ipl.org/ - The Internet Public Library is exactly what it sounds like – an online reference collection.

http://www.loc.gov - This link is the gateway to the Library of Congress. The Library of Congress is the largest library in the world, with more than 120 million items.

http://www.apa.org/journals/webref.html - The American Psychological Association's guide to citing online sources.

http://www.uvm.edu/~xli/reference/mla.html - Modern Language Association guide to citing online sources.

CHAPTER 14: Organizing

Interactive Chapter Outline

I. Outlining the Body of the Speech

_____

_____

A. Writing a Thesis Statement

_____

_____

B. Outlining Main Points

_____

_____

C. Revise Main Points

_____

_____

_____

_____

214

D. Determining the Best Order

_____

_____

_____

_____

II. Selecting and Outlining Supporting Material

_____

_____

A. List Supporting Material

_____

_____

III. Outlining Section Transitions

_____

_____

IV. Preparing the Introduction

_____

_____

A. Goals of the Introduction

_____

_____

_____

_____

B. Types of Introductions

_____

_____

_____

_____

_____

_____

V. Preparing the Conclusion

_____

_____

    A. Types of Conclusions

_____

_____

_____

_____

VI. Listing Sources

_____

_____

VII. Completing the Outline

_____

_____

_____

_____

Key Terms

thesis statement (p. 336)

_____

_____

main points (p. 337)

216

clarity of main points (p. 339)

parallel structure of main points (p. 339)

meaningful main points (p. 340)

limited number of main points (p. 340)

topic order (p. 341)

time or chronological order (p. 342)

logical reasons order (p. 342)

transitions (p. 345)

section transitions (p. 345)

rhetorical question (p. 348)

appeal (p. 351)

Exercises
Journal Activities

Journal Activity 14.1 – Writing Thesis Statements (p. 327)

1. Write your tentative speech goal. For instance, Emming's goal was, "I want the audience to be able to find the credit card that is most suitable for them."

2. List the elements of your speech goal that might become the main points of your speech. For instance, Emming's were interest rate, convenience, discounts, annual fee, rebates, institutional reputation, and frequent flyer points.

📖 Journal Activity 14.1 – Writing Thesis Statements (cont.)

3. Evaluate the topics on your list and select the specific elements that best reflect your speech goal.

4. Combine these main points into a complete sentence that will be your thesis statement.

📖 Journal Activity 14.2 – Outlining the Speech Body (p. 347)

Outline the body of your first speech.

1. Write the speech goal at the top of the page.
2. Write the thesis statement next.
3. Select the headings (main points) from your thesis statement.
-Write the perspective main points in outline form.
-Revise the wording of the main points so that each is written in a complete sentence that is clear, parallel and meaningful.
-Based on the nature of the material and your audience, determine the best order for the main points: topic order, time order, or logical reasons order. If need be, rewrite the main point sin this order.
4. List the factual statements, expert opinions, and other information you have found to develop each main point.
-Group the points of information that relate to each other.
-Subordinate material so that each subpoint contains only one idea.
5. Write transition statements in the body of the outline that summarize the previous main point or forecast the next main point.

Journal Activity 14.2 – Outlining the Speech Body (cont.)

Speech Goal: _____

Thesis Statement: _____

Main points, subpoints, supporting information and transitions:

Journal Activity 14.2 – Outlining the Speech Body (cont.)

📖 Journal Activity 14.3 – Writing Speech Introductions (p. 350)

Prepare three separate introductions that you believe would be appropriate for the body of the speech you outlines in Journal Activity 14.2, and present them aloud. Then write answers to the following questions: Which do you believe is the best? Why?

Journal Activity 14.3 – Writing Speech Introductions (cont.)

📖 Journal Activity 14.4 – Writing Speech Conclusions (p. 352)

Prepare three separate conclusions that you believe would be appropriate for the body of the speech you outlines in Journal Activity 14.2, and present them aloud. Then write answers to the following questions: Which do you believe is the best? Why?

224

📖 Journal Activity 14.4 – Writing Speech Conclusions (cont.)

📖 Journal Activity 14.5 – Completing the Speech Outline (p. 355)

Using the information form the previous four journal activities, complete the sentence outline for the first speech. Include your sources at the end of the outline.

Compare what you have written to the sample outline (Figure 14.2 on pages 356-357) to make sure that it conforms to the guidelines discussed in chapter 14. Make sure you have included your speech goal, a thesis statement, an introduction, clearly written main points, transitions between main points, a conclusion, and a list of sources. You may write the outline in the space provided below, download an informative speech outline and organization form from the websites listed in the "Useful and Interesting Internet Links" section of this chapter or use the paper copies at the end of this chapter.

Complete Speech Outline:

📖 Journal Activity 14.5 – Completing the Speech Outline (cont.)

14.6 Using InfoTrac College Edition (p. 346)

Using InfoTrac College Edition, click on Power Trac. Press on Key Word and drag down to Journal Name. Enter "Vital Speeches." View Vital Speeches and find Johnson, Geneva B. "Service: Life beyond self."

1. What is her speech goal?

2. Outline her main points. Were they clearly stated? If not, how might she have increased their clarity? If so, what led to their clarity?

3. Identify any transitions between main points. Which transition(s) seemed particularly informative or useful? Why?

4. How does she conclude her speech? What goals does her conclusion meet?

14.7 Using InfoTrac College Edition (p. 352)
Using InfoTrac College Edition, click on Power Trac. Press on Key Word and drag down to Journal Name. Enter "Vital Speeches." View Vital Speeches and identify three speeches to look at; then view those speeches. Read and analyze the introductions and conclusions to those speeches. Which ones meet the goals discussed in this chapter? What could the speakers have done to make the introductions and conclusions better? What qualities, if any, did you find helpful in preparing your introduction and conclusion?

14.8 Using the Web
Locate a web site of quotations. Browse the site. Seek quotes relevant to your speech and write a few in the space below. How may these be used to enhance your introduction and/or conclusion? (Be sure to copy full bibliographic information concerning the source of the quote.)

14.9 What Would You Do? (p. 358)
Read the *What Would You Do: A Question of Ethics* scenario on page 358 of your text. Answer the following questions in the space provided here.

1. What are the ethical issues here?

2. Is anyone really hurt by Marna opening the speech with this story?

3. What are the speaker's ethical responsibilities?

14.10 Outline A Sample Speech

Outline a professor's lecture in one of your other classes. Critique the outline based on the recommendations in Chapter 14 of your text. Write a summary of your critique below. Focus on the following questions: What was the pattern of organization? Was the lecture easy to follow? Why or why not? Were transitions used? If so, provide an example. Was a distinct and clear introduction and conclusion part of the lecture? Were any of the methods discussed in Chapter 14 used in the introduction or conclusion?

Chapter 14 Quiz Questions (answers and page references in Appendix)

True/False

1. Transition statements should not be placed in the outline.

2. Topic order organizes the main ideas of a speech by categories or divisions.

3. Main points should be written as complete sentences.

4. Using a rhetorical question in the introduction is a poor idea because as the audience ponders the answer to the question, they will not be paying attention to the speech.

5. The appeal to action ends a persuasive speech.

Multiple Choice

1. A thesis statement
    a. is a sentence that outlines the elements of the specific goal statement
    b. is the same as the specific goal statement
    c. should be written after the introduction
    d. is not necessary in a well-organized speech

2. Main points should be
    a. clear
    b. written in parallel structure format
    c. limited to five or fewer in number
    d. meaningful
    e. all of the above

3. Danny organizes his speech on changing the oil in a car with main ideas that are the steps in the process. His speech is organized using what order?
    a. time order
    b. logical reasons order
    c. problem-solution order
    d. topic order

4. At the end of her first main idea, Alexandra says: "Now that we have seen the causes of credit card debt, lets look at what we can do about it." You recognize this sentence as a:
    a. conclusion
    b. main point
    c. transition
    d. attention getter

5. You are listening to a speech that starts off with the following: "What would you do if you won the lottery today? Would you spend the money? Would you save it? Would you donate it?" You recognize this as what type of introduction?
> a. startling statement
> b. rhetorical question
> c. reference
> d. emotional impact
> e. parallel structure

Essay

1. Discuss the several different goals of an introduction and at least three different ways of achieving those goals.

2. What are three different ways of organizing a speech and provide an example of each.

Useful and Interesting Internet Links

http://www.public-speaking.org/public-speaking-articles.htm#organization - A set of articles on organization from the Advanced Public Speaking Institute.

http://www.ukans.edu/cwis/units/coms2/vpa/vpa6.htm - Tips on outlining from the Virtual Presentation Assistant of the University of Kansas.

http://www.vscc.cc.tn.us/dew/103inftime.htm
http://www.vscc.cc.tn.us/dew/103inftopical.htm
http://www.vscc.cc.tn.us/dew/103perlogicalreasons.htm - These three links provide access to sample outline "templates" for time order, topic order and logical reasons order speeches. They can be useful in visualizing an outline for these types of speeches.

http://www.ifas.ufl.edu/~nee3030/orgout.html - This site from the University of Florida is designed to assist students in developing and organizing speech outlines.

http://www.duke.edu/~de1/evaluate.html - How to evaluate the quality of evidence in speeches.

Organization and Outline Forms for Informative Speeches

Time Order

Title: _____

Specific Goal: _____

INTRODUCTION

I. _____

_____

_____

II. _____

_____

Attention-getting material:_____

_____

Material to relate importance of plan to audience's interests:

_____

Preview of the steps:_____

_____

Thesis Statement: _____

_____

BODY

I. Main point (step 1 or 1st event)_____

  A. Major point (to explain step 1 or event 1)_____

    1. Support (a statistic, narrative, example, definition, testimony, or comparison)_____

    2. Support (a statistic, narrative, example, definition, testimony, or comparison)_____

  B. Major point (to explain step 1 or event 1)_____

    1. Support (a statistic, narrative, example, definition, testimony, or comparison)_____

    2. Support (a statistic, narrative, example, definition, testimony, or comparison)_____

  C. Major point (to explain step 1 or event 1)_____

    1. Support (a statistic, narrative, example, definition, testimony, or comparison)_____

    2. Support (a statistic, narrative, example, definition, testimony, or comparison)_____

Transition to second main point

_____

II. Main point (step 2 or 2nd event)_____

  A. Major point (to explain step 2 or event 2))_____

    1. Support (a statistic, narrative, example, definition, testimony, or comparison)_____

    2. Support (a statistic, narrative, example, definition, testimony, or comparison)_____

  B. Major point (to explain step 2 or event 2)_____

    1. Support (a statistic, narrative, example, definition, testimony, or comparison)_____

    2. Support (a statistic, narrative, example, definition, testimony, or comparison)_____

  C. Major point (to explain step 2 or event 2)_____

    1. Support (a statistic, narrative, example, definition, testimony, or comparison)_____

2. Support (a statistic, narrative, example, definition, testimony, or comparison)_____

Transition to third main point

_____   ___

III. Main point (step 3 or 3rd event)_____

   A. Major point (to explain step 3 or event 3)_____

      1. Support (a statistic, narrative, example, definition, testimony, or comparison)_____

      2. Support (a statistic, narrative, example, definition, testimony, or comparison)_____

   B. Major point (to explain step 3 or event 3)_____

      1. Support (a statistic, narrative, example, definition, testimony, or comparison)_____

      2. Support (a statistic, narrative, example, definition, testimony, or comparison)_____

   C. Major point (to explain step 3 or event 3)_____

      1. Support (a statistic, narrative, example, definition, testimony, or comparison)_____

      2. Support (a statistic, narrative, example, definition, testimony, or comparison)_____

CONCLUSION

I. _____

_____

II. _____

_____

Summary of Steps or Events_____

236

Concluding remarks _____

SOURCES

TOPICAL ORDER

Title:_____

Specific Goal:_____

INTRODUCTION

I. _____

_____

_____

II. _____

_____

Attention-getting material:_____

_____

Material to relate importance to audience's interests:

_____

Preview of the categories:_____

_____

Thesis Statement: _____

_____

BODY

I. Main point (first category)_____

   A. Major point (to explain category)_____

      1. Support (a statistic, narrative, example, definition,
        testimony, or comparison)_____

      2. Support (a statistic, narrative, example, definition,

testimony, or comparison)_____

B. Major point (to explain category)_____

    1. Support (a statistic, narrative, example, definition, testimony, or comparison)_____

    2. Support (a statistic, narrative, example, definition, testimony, or comparison)_____

C. Major point (to explain category)_____

    1. Support (a statistic, narrative, example, definition, testimony, or comparison)_____

    2. Support (a statistic, narrative, example, definition, testimony, or comparison)_____

Transition to second main point

_____

II. Main point (second category)_____

A. Major point (to explain category)_____
    1. Support (a statistic, narrative, example, definition, testimony, or comparison)_____

    2. Support (a statistic, narrative, example, definition, testimony, or comparison)_____

B. Major point (to explain category)_____

    1. Support (a statistic, narrative, example, definition, testimony, or comparison)_____

    2. Support (a statistic, narrative, example, definition, testimony, or comparison)_____

C. Major point (to explain category)_____

    1. Support (a statistic, narrative, example, definition, testimony, or comparison)_____

    2. Support (a statistic, narrative, example, definition, testimony, or comparison)_____

Transition to third main point

_____

III. Main point (third category)_____

   A. Major point (to explain category)_____
      1. Support (a statistic, narrative, example, definition,
         testimony, or comparison)_____

      2. Support (a statistic, narrative, example, definition,
         testimony, or comparison)_____

   B. Major point (to explain category)_____

      1. Support (a statistic, narrative, example, definition,
         testimony, or comparison)_____

      2. Support (a statistic, narrative, example, definition,
         testimony, or comparison)_____

   C. Major point (to explain category)_____

      1. Support (a statistic, narrative, example, definition,
         testimony, or comparison)_____

      2. Support (a statistic, narrative, example, definition,
         testimony, or comparison)_____

CONCLUSION

I. _____

_____

II. _____

_____

Summary of categories (groups, topics, or clusters)_____

_____

240

Concluding remarks_____

_____

SOURCES

Statement of Logical Reasons

Title:_____

Specific Goal:_____

INTRODUCTION

I. _____

_____

_____

II. _____

_____

Thesis Statement: _____

_____

BODY

I. Main point (the problem is...)_____

  A. Major point (history of the problem)_____

    1. Subpoint (the problem started when...)_____

      a. Support (a statistic, narrative, example, definition, testimony, or comparison)_____

      b. Support (a statistic, narrative, example, definition, testimony, or comparison)_____

    2. Subpoint (the problem started because...)_____

      a. Support (a statistic, narrative, example, definition, testimony, or comparison)_____

      b. Support (a statistic, narrative, example, definition, testimony, or comparison)_____

    3. Subpoint (the problem is extensive)_____

       a. Support (a statistic, narrative, example, definition, testimony, or comparison)_____

       b. Support (a statistic, narrative, example, definition, testimony, or comparison)_____

  B. Major point (the problem is harmful)_____

    1. Subpoint (the specific harms are several)_____

       a. Subpoint (harm 1 is...)_____

       b. Subpoint (harm 2 is...)_____

       c. Subpoint (harm 3 is...)_____

    2. Subpoint (the harms will continue or increase unless we make a change)_____

       a. Support (a statistic, narrative, example, definition, testimony, or comparison)_____

       b. Support (a statistic, narrative, example, definition, testimony, or comparison)_____

Transition to second main point

_____

II. Main point (the solution is...)_____

  A. Major point (the solution will solve the problem)_____

    1. Subpoint (it is practical)_____

       a. Support (a statistic, narrative, example, definition, testimony, or comparison)_____

       b. Support (a statistic, narrative, example, definition, testimony, or comparison)_____

    2. Subpoint (it is feasible)_____

       a. Support (a statistic, narrative, example, definition,

testimony, or comparison)_____

    b. Support (a statistic, narrative, example, definition, testimony, or comparison)_____

B. Major point (the solution can be accomplished)_____

    1. Subpoint (the plan is to proceed this way)_____

      a. Step 1 is:_____

      b. Step 2 is:_____

      c. Step 3 is:_____

    2. Subpoint (who will put the plan into operation)_____

      a. Subpoint (their competence is known)_____

        (1) Support _____

        (2) Support _____.

      b. Subpoint (audience members must do this...)_____

      _____

CONCLUSION

I. _____

_____

II. _____

_____

SOURCES

CHAPTER 15: Adapting Verbally and Visually

Learning Objectives

After studying this chapter, you should be able to answer the following questions:

- What can you do to develop common ground?
- What can you do to create or build audience interest?
- What can you do to adapt to your audience's level of understanding?
- What can you do to build the audience's perception of you as a speaker?
- What can you do to reinforce or change an audience's attitude toward your topic?
- What criteria do you use to select and construct visual aids?
- What do you include in an audience adaptation strategy?

Interactive Chapter Outline

i. Developing Common Ground

_____

_____

A. Use Personal Pronouns

_____

_____

B. Ask Rhetorical Questions

_____

_____

C. Share Common Experiences

_____

_____

D. Personalize Information

_____

_____

II. Creating and Maintaining Audience Interest

_____

_____

A. Timeliness

_____

_____

B. Proximity

_____

_____

C. Seriousness

_____

_____

D. Vividness

_____

_____

III. Adapting to Audience Level of Understanding

_____

_____

A. Orienting Listeners

_____

_____

B. Presenting New Information

_____

_____

246

_____

_____

IV. Building a Positive Attitude Toward You as a Speaker

_____

_____

  A. Building Audience Perception of Your Knowledge and Expertise

  _____

  _____

  B. Building Audience Perception of Your Trustworthiness

  _____

  _____

  C. Building Audience Perception of Your Personality

  _____

  _____

V. Adapting to Audience Attitude Toward Your Speech Goal

  _____

  _____

  A. Special Problems of Speakers from Different Cultures

  _____

  _____

VI. Adapting to Audiences Visually

  _____

  _____

  A. Visual Aids You Can Carry

_____

_____

_____

_____

_____

_____

B. Visual Aids You Can Create

_____

_____

_____

_____

C. Media for Showing Visual Aids

_____

_____

_____

_____

D. Designing Drawings, Overheads, and Computer Projections

_____

_____

_____

_____

_____

_____

248

E. Making Choices

_____

_____

VII. A plan of Adaptation

_____

_____

_____

_____

A. Audience Analysis

_____

_____

B. Speech Plan

_____

_____

Key Terms

audience adaptation (p. 362)

_____

_____

common ground (p. 362)

_____

_____

personal pronouns (p. 362)

_____

_____

rhetorical questions (p. 363)

_____

_____

personalize (p. 363)

_____

_____

timely (p. 363)

_____

_____

proximity (p. 366)

_____

_____

serious (p. 367)

_____

_____

vivid (p. 367)

_____

_____

credibility (p. 370)

_____

_____

trustworthiness (p. 371)

_____

_____

attitude (p. 372)

_____

_____

visual aid (p. 375)

_____

_____

chart (p. 377)

_____

_____

word chart (p. 377)

_____

_____

organizational chart (p. 378)

_____

_____

graph (p. 378)

_____

_____

bar graph (p. 378)

_____

_____

line graph (p. 378)

_____

_____

pie graph (p. 379)

_____

_____

speech plan (p. 386)

_____

_____

Exercises
Journal Activities

Journal Activity 15.1 – Selecting Visual Aids (p. 386)

1. Carefully study the verbal information you are planning to use in the speech. Indicate below *where* you believe visual aids would be effective in creating audience interest, facilitating understanding, or increasing retention. Limit your choices to four or five spots at most, since your time limits for a first speech are likely to be four to six minutes.

2. Now indicate *which kind* of visual aids would be most effective in each of the places you have identified: Yourself? Objects? Models? Charts? Pictorial Representations? Projections? Chalkboard? Handouts? Computer Graphics?

3. Finally, indicate specifics for the visual aids themselves. For instance, if you have elected to use a chart for one place, what are you likely to put on it?

📖 Journal Activity 15.2 – A Speech Plan for Adapting to the Audience (p. 388)

In Journal Activity 12.2, you wrote an audience analysis for your first speech that looked like Emming's, shown in Figure 15.3 on page 388 of your text. Now, write a speech plan and an audience adaptation strategy, in which you include specifics about how you will adapt to your audience using information that you included in Activity 12.2. Emming's plan, shown in Figure 15.4 on page 388 of your text, may be used as a model. Incorporate the headings indicated below. Where appropriate, include discussion of your visual aids.

Speech Plan:
1. Common Ground

2. Audience Interest

3. Audience Understanding

4. Audience Attitude Toward the Speaker

5. Audience Attitude Toward the Speech Goal

15.3 Using InfoTrac College Edition (p. 363)

Click on Power Trac. Press on Key Word and drag down to Journal Name. Enter "Vital Speeches." View Vital Speeches and find a speech on or related to your topic, and read that speech. Look for ways the speaker attempted to create common ground. Did the speaker use personal pronouns or rhetorical questions? Share common experiences? Personalize information? If you find many examples, how did they help make the speech better? If you found few examples, how would their use have made the speech better?

15.4 Using InfoTrac College Edition

Using InfoTrac College Edition, do a subject search using the term "visual aids." Go to Periodical References and find the article titled "The effect of a nonverbal aid on preschoolers' recall for color, " by Ling and Blades. (*Journal of Genetic Psychology*, Sept 2000.) Read the article and summarize the findings below. How do the research findings presented relate to the use of visual aids in speeches?

254

15.5 Using Technology (p. 367)

Watch two workout videos: one made specifically for novices and the other for fitness buffs. Focus on the talk, not the workout. Note the difference in the way trainers speak to their intended audiences. What guidelines for adaptation can you draw from this experience?

15.6 Using Technology

Go to http://einstein.cs.uri.edu/tutorials/csc101/powerpoint/ppt.html and review the basics for using Microsoft PowerPoint software. (If you prefer or if you have different presentation software available at your home or school, use an Internet search engine such as Yahoo! or Dogpile to find an online tutorial for your software of choice.) Presentation software can be useful in creating computerized presentations, overheads, slide shows and/or handouts. Using the tutorial, teach yourself the basics of the program and design a possible visual aid for your speech. How can a visual aid of this type influence the audience's attitude toward the speaker?

15.7 Preparing a Handout

Prepare a one-page handout on "Mistakes to Avoid When Using Visual Aids." The audience will be your speech class. The handout should be clear, visually appealing, focus on main points and reflect an understanding of the material covered in Chapter 15 of your text. Be prepared to discuss and present your handout to your classmates.

15.8 Analyzing Visual Aids

Using the handout designed in exercise 15.7 or one you have prepared for your first speech, analyze it using the following checklist. Considering your analysis, would you make any changes to your visual aid? If so, what would they be?

15.8 Analyzing Visual Aids (cont.)

Visual Aid Assessment Check List:

	Excellent (A)	Good (B)	Average (C)	Poor (D)
Type of visual aid is suited to the audience				
Aid is visually pleasing overall				
Size of type is appropriate and pleasing to the eye.				
Both upper and lower case type used				
Limit the number of phrases to six				
Focus on information that is emphasized in the speech				
Color and/or clip art, if used, enhances impact				

15.9 Graphing Numerical Data

Locate an article in a journal, newspaper or magazine that presents data in numerical form. (You may choose to use InfoTrac College Edition or the Internet to locate a suitable article.) After you have examined the numerical data, decide how to represent that data visually. After you have decided, create an appropriate chart. You may decide to create your chart using PowerPoint or other appropriate software. After you create your visual, us a copy of the Visual Aid Assessment Check List to evaluate the quality of your visual. Be prepared to share your visual with your classmates.

Visual Aid Assessment Check List:

	Excellent (A)	Good (B)	Average (C)	Poor (D)
Type of visual aid is suited to the audience				
Aid is visually pleasing overall				
Size of type is appropriate and pleasing to the eye.				
Both upper and lower case type used				
Limit the number of phrases to six				
Focus on information that is emphasized in the speech				
Color and/or clip art, if used, enhances impact				

15.10 What Would You Do? (p. 389)
Read the *What Would You Do: A Question of Ethics* scenario on page 389 of your text.
Answer the following questions in the space provided here.

1. In a speech, is it ethical to adapt in a way that resonates with your audience but isn't in keeping with what you really believe? Why or why not?

2. Could Kendra have achieved her goal using a different method? How?

Chapter 15 Quiz Questions (answers and page references in Appendix)

True/False

1. A speech plan is a written strategy for developing a thesis statement and topic sentence.

2. Since chalkboards are usually large, they are best suited for larger, more complex visual aids that take time to be written down.

3. The best visual aids are simple –uncluttered and easy to see.

4. It is best to not use vivid language, as such language tends to arouse the senses of the audience.

5. Personality is usually not an issue with speakers, as the audience cannot tell much from a speaker's nonverbal cues.

Multiple Choice

1.   Vladimir is doing a speech on his native country of Russia. He decides to dress in traditional Russian clothing for his speech. This could be an example of
    a. using models as a visual aid
    b. using objects as a visual aid
    c. using yourself as a visual aid
    d. establishing common ground
    e. none of the above

2. In her speech, Karen says: "Over 100,000 people a year die of this disease.   That's twice the population of this town and five times the population of this college!" This is an example of
    a. developing common ground through personalizing information
    b. developing common ground by sharing a common experience
    c. adapting to the audience visually
    d. the use of proximity

3. "The level of trust an audience has or will have in the speaker" is the definition of
    a. attitude
    b. credibility
    c. audience analysis
    d. trustworthiness
    e. none of the above

4. A diagram that shows relationships among parts of a single unit is called
    a. a bar graph
    b. a line graph
    c. an organizational chart
    d. a pie graph

5. Christina wishes to compare the market share of two different soft drink companies to each other. The most appropriate visual aid to do this would be
    a. a bar graph
    b. a pie graph
    c. a line chart
    d. a photograph
    e. a proximity graph

Essay

1. Discuss several ways in which a speaker may build her or his credibility with an audience.

2. What are the different types of visual aids and how can visual aids help improve a speech?

Useful and Interesting Internet Links

http://www.public-speaking.org/public-speaking-articles.htm - The Advanced Public Speaking Institute contains a series of articles on the use of visual aids.

http://www.ukans.edu/cwis/units/coms2/vpa/vpa7.htm - Tips on using visual aids from the Virtual Presentation Assistant at the University of Kansas.

http://sorrel.humboldt.edu/~jmf2/floss/visual-aids.html - Types of visual aids and tips for using them, with some Internet-based examples.

http://www.fastcompany.com/online/07/130crash.html - Tips on giving a "catastrophe free" presentation when using visual aids and technology.

http://einstein.cs.uri.edu/tutorials/csc101/powerpoint/ppt.html - An online tutorial for using Microsoft PowerPoint presentation software.

http://www.presentations.com/ - Presentations.com is an online magazine devoted to presentations, public speaking and visual aids. They offer a free subscription.

CHAPTER 16: Practicing the Presentation of Your Speech

Learning Objectives

After studying this chapter, you should be able to answer the following questions:

- What is extemporaneous speaking?
- What elements of language are most relevant to public speaking?
- What characteristics result in conversational quality?
- What are the characteristics of effective speech practice?
- What are comforting ideas about speaker nervousness?
- What are specific behaviors for limiting nervousness?
- By what criteria is an effective speech measured?

Interactive Chapter Outline

I. Components to Practice in Your Speech

_____

_____

   A. Verbal Components

_____

_____

   B. Nonverbal Components

_____

_____

_____

_____

II. Achieving a Conversational Quality

_____

_____

A. Enthusiasm

_____

_____

B. Vocal Effectiveness

_____

_____

C. Spontaneity

_____

_____

D. Fluency

_____

_____

E. Eye Contact

_____

_____

III. Rehearsal

_____

_____

A. Timetable for Preparation and Practice

_____

_____

B. Using Notes in Your Speech

_____

_____

C. Using Visual Aids in Your Speech

_____

_____

D. Guidelines for Effective Rehearsal

_____

_____

IV. Coping with Nervousness

_____

_____

_____

_____

A. Specific Behaviors

_____

_____

_____

_____

_____

_____

B. Persistent Nervousness

_____

_____

V. Criteria for Evaluating Speeches

_____

_____

_____

_____

Key Terms

extemporaneous speech (p. 394)

_____

_____

simile (p. 395)

_____

_____

metaphor (p. 395)

_____

_____

emphasis (p. 395)

_____

_____

emphasis by proportion (p. 395)

_____

_____

emphasis by repeating (p. 395)

_____

_____

emphasis by transition (p. 395)

_____

_____

voice (p. 396)

_____

_____

articulation (p. 397)

_____

_____

pronunciation (p. 397)

_____

_____

bodily action (p. 397)

_____

_____

facial expressions (p. 397)

_____

_____

gestures (p. 397)

_____

_____

posture (p. 398)

_____

_____

movement (p. 398)

_____

_____

poise (p. 398)

_____

_____

conversational quality (p. 400)

_____

_____

266

enthusiasm (p. 400)

_____

_____

vocal expressiveness (p. 400)

_____

_____

monotone (p. 400)

_____

_____

spontaneity (p. 402)

_____

_____

fluency (p. 402)

_____

_____

eye contact (p. 403)

_____

_____

rehearsing (p. 403)

_____

_____

speech notes (p. 406)

_____

_____

learning the speech (p. 409)

_____

_____

nervousness (p. 410)

visualization (p. 414)

systematic desensitization (p. 416)

cognitive restructuring (p. 416)

Exercises
Journal Activities

Journal Activity 16.1 – Similes and Metaphors (p. 395)

As you read newspapers and magazine articles and listen to people talk over the next few days, make note of both trite and original similes and metaphors. In the space below, write at least three that you thought were particularly well used. Then briefly indicate how and why they impressed you.

Simile/Metaphor #1

Simile/Metaphor #2

Simile/Metaphor #3

Journal Activity 16.2 – Rehearsal Log (p. 410)

Keep a separate log for each time you practiced your speech aloud and standing up as if facing your audience.

For your first practice, indicate how long you spoke. Then write two or three sentences focusing on what went well and what you need to improve.

For each additional speech practice, indicate where in the speech you made changes to build interest, clarify points, and build a positive attitude toward you and your topic. Also, indicate where you made changes to improve language, delivery, and use of visual aids.

Finally, answer the following questions: How many times did you practice aloud for this speech? When did you feel you had mastery of the ideas of the speech?

(You may use the space below to answer the questions and the rehearsal logs that follow to record your progress.)

Journal Activity 16.2 – Rehearsal Log cont.)

Speech Rehearsal Log

Speech #: _____ , Rehearsal #: _____

Length of Speech: _____ (minutes and seconds)

<u>I. What went well?</u>

<u>II. What needs improvement?</u>

<u>III. Changes to:</u>
Build interest:

Clarify points:

Build a positive attitude toward speaker and topic:

Improve language:

Improve delivery:

Improve use of visual aids:

Speech Rehearsal Log

Speech #: _____, Rehearsal #: _____

Length of Speech: _____ (minutes and seconds)

<u>I. What went well?</u>

<u>II. What needs improvement?</u>

<u>III. Changes to:</u>
Build interest:

Clarify points:

Build a positive attitude toward speaker and topic:

Improve language:

Improve delivery:

Improve use of visual aids:

Journal Activity 16.3 – Controlling Nervousness (p. 416)

Interview one or two people who give frequent speeches (a minister, a politician, a lawyer, a businessperson, a teacher.) Ask what is likely to make them more or less nervous about giving a speech. Find out how they cope with their nervousness. Summarize the results of interviews below. Then write which behaviors you believe might work for you?

16.4 Using InfoTrac College Edition (p. 414)

Visualization has been recognized as a means of improving performance in many areas, most specifically in athletics. Open InfoTrac and type in key word "visualization." You will find many recent sources covering many different areas. Look for "Do try this at home," In *Women's Sports and Fitness*, May 1997, and "The mind of a champion," *Natural Health*, Jan-Feb. 1997. Look specifically for suggested procedures for using visualization. Summarize them here.

16.5 Using InfoTrac College Edition

Using InfoTrac College Edition, locate and read the article "Breaking the language barrier," by Stephanie Nickerson. (You can use Power Trac to search by author or do a key word search using the author's name.) Answer the following questions.

1. Under what speaking circumstances is it important to speak clearly and slowly?

2. Describe one suggestion offered in the article to slow down your rate of speech.

3. Why do you think Nickerson advocates not apologizing to an audience for speech habits and accents? Do you feel you have any such habits?

16.6 Using Technology (p. 409)

Arrange to videotape yourself rehearsing your speech. As you review the videotape, focus on your enthusiasm, vocal expressiveness, fluency, spontaneity, and eye contact. Identify the sections where your delivery was particularly effective and the sections where you need to improve. Then practice the sections that you believe need the most work. After a few run throughs, rerecord those sections of the speech. You will be pleased with the improvement.

<u>16.7 What Would You Do? (p. 423)</u>
Read the *What Would You Do: A Question of Ethics* scenario on page 423 of your text. Answer the following questions in the space provided here.

1. Now that Megan knows Donnell doesn't care for Terry, should she let him give the speech? Why?

2. And what about Donnell? Should he give such a speech knowing that he wouldn't support Terry himself? Why?

<u>16.8 Thinking About Voice and Articulation Problems (p. 397)</u>
Indicate what you regard as your major problem of voice and articulation (such as speaking in a monotone or slurring words). Outline a plan for working on the problem.

16.9 Thinking About Nervousness (p. 413)

Are you nervous at the thought of giving a speech? What thoughts and behaviors show your nervousness? What can you do to control your nervousness?

16.10 Speech Analysis

Use the Speech Critique Sheet on the following page to analyze the sample speech provided in your textbook on pages 421-423. While you are reading the speech, cover the right side of the page so you are unable to see the author's analysis. When your analysis is complete, compare your results to that of the authors. Where do you agree with their analysis? Where do you disagree?

(Note: You will be unable to evaluate the speaker on some aspects of presentation as the speech is in written, not verbal form.)

(Note: You may use this form to also evaluate a recorded version of your own speech or one of the speeches provided on the *Communicate!* CD-ROM provided with your text. An extra copy of the form is provided here for that purpose.)

Diagnostic Speech Checklist

(Check all items that were done effectively.)

Content:
_____ 1. Was the goal of the speech clear?
_____ 2. Did the speaker have high-quality information?
_____ 3. Did the speaker use a variety of kinds of developmental material?
_____ 4. Were visual aids appropriate and well used?
_____ 5. Did speaker establish common ground and adapt content to the audience?

Organization:
_____ 6. Did the introduction gain attention, goodwill and lead into the body?
_____ 7. Were the main points clear, parallel and meaningful?
_____ 8. Did transitions lead smoothly from one point to another?
_____ 9. Did the conclusion tie the speech together?

Presentation:
_____ 10. Was the language clear?
_____ 11. Was the language vivid?
_____ 12. Was the language emphatic?
_____ 13. Did the speaker sound enthusiastic?
_____ 14. Was the speaker vocally expressive?
_____ 15. Was the presentation spontaneous?
_____ 16. Was the presentation fluent?
_____ 17. Did the speaker look at the audience?
_____ 18. Were pronunciation and articulation acceptable?
_____ 19. Did the speaker have good posture?
_____ 20. Was speaker movement appropriate?
_____ 21. Did the speaker have sufficient poise?

Comments:

Based on these criteria, evaluate the speech as (check one):

_____ excellent, _____ good, _____ satisfactory, _____ fair, _____ poor.

Diagnostic Speech Checklist

(Check all items that were done effectively.)

Content:
_____ 1. Was the goal of the speech clear?
_____ 2. Did the speaker have high-quality information?
_____ 3. Did the speaker use a variety of kinds of developmental material?
_____ 4. Were visual aids appropriate and well used?
_____ 5. Did speaker establish common ground and adapt content to the audience?

Organization:
_____ 6. Did the introduction gain attention, goodwill and lead into the body?
_____ 7. Were the main points clear, parallel and meaningful?
_____ 8. Did transitions lead smoothly from one point to another?
_____ 9. Did the conclusion tie the speech together?

Presentation:
_____ 10. Was the language clear?
_____ 11. Was the language vivid?
_____ 12. Was the language emphatic?
_____ 13. Did the speaker sound enthusiastic?
_____ 14. Was the speaker vocally expressive?
_____ 15. Was the presentation spontaneous?
_____ 16. Was the presentation fluent?
_____ 17. Did the speaker look at the audience?
_____ 18. Were pronunciation and articulation acceptable?
_____ 19. Did the speaker have good posture?
_____ 20. Was speaker movement appropriate?
_____ 21. Did the speaker have sufficient poise?

Comments:

Based on these criteria, evaluate the speech as (check one):

_____ excellent, _____ good, _____ satisfactory, _____ fair, _____ poor.

Chapter 16 Quiz Questions (answers and page references in Appendix)

True/False

1. Since being nervous is natural, there is no way to cope with it.

2. "A style of presentation that sounds like a conversation to listeners" is the definition of extemporaneous speech.

3. A monotone voice can actually lull an audience to sleep.

4. Since notes detract from eye contact, they should not be used.

5. You should talk about your visual aid while showing it.

Multiple Choice

1. The statement "The snow covered the city like a blanket" is an example of a(n)
    a. simile
    b. metaphor
    c. transition
    d. parallelism
    e. precision

2. Saying "libary" instead of "library" is an error in
    a. articulation
    b. precision
    c. pronunciation
    d. expressiveness

3. How can we develop spontaneity in our speeches?
    a. make our speech devoid of hesitations
    b. use vivid language
    c. add emphasis
    d. get to know the ideas in our speech
    e. none of the above

4. How many three-by-five note cards would normally be sufficient for a six-to-eight minute speech?
    a. one or two
    b. three or four
    c. six or seven
    d. eight or nine

5. What are the three major areas of emphasis for evaluating speeches?

a. content, organization, and presentation
b. content, organization and nervousness
c. content, presentation and articulation
d. articulation, emphasis and vividness

Essay

1. Discuss why it is important to achieve a conversational quality to your speeches and the five different components of conversational quality.

2. Discuss some guidelines for using visual aids in a speech. Focus on using the aid, not creating it.

Useful and Interesting Internet Links

http://www.webofculture.com/worldsmart/gestures.html - Information on the ways in which body language and gestures are interpreted by different cultures from "The Web of Culture."

http://www.ljlseminars.com/bodyspeaks.htm - A discussion of the impact of speaker's body language on the audience.

http://www.public-speaking.org/public-speaking-articles.htm#practice - Articles on practicing from the Advanced Public Speaking Institute.

http://www.public-speaking.org/public-speaking-articles.htm#stage - Articles on stage fright from the Advanced Public Speaking Institute.

http://www.public-speaking.org/public-speaking-setupchecklist-article.htm - A room setup checklist from the Advanced Public Speaking Institute.

http://www.ukans.edu/cwis/units/coms2/vpa/vpa8.htm - Guidelines and links to help present your speech effectively from the University of Kansas' Virtual Presentation Assistant.

http://www.speechtips.com/delivering.html - Tips on delivery from Speechtips.com. (To go to the main page: http://www.speechtips.com)

CHAPTER 17: Informative Speaking

Learning Objectives

After studying this chapter, you should be able to answer the following questions:

- What are the three goals of informative speaking?
- What are the tests of presenting ideas creatively?
- What can you do to increase your credibility?
- How can you proceed to leave the impression that what you have said is new and relevant?
- What key techniques can you use to emphasize information?
- What are the major methods of informing?
- What are the key criteria for evaluating an informative speech?

Interactive Chapter Outline

I. Principles of Informing

_____

_____

A. Credibility

_____

_____

B. Intellectual Stimulation

_____

_____

C. Creativity

_____

_____

_____

_____

D. Relevance

_____

_____

E. Emphasis

_____

_____

_____

_____

_____

II. Methods of Informing

_____

_____

A. Narrating

_____

_____

B. Describing

_____

_____

C. Defining

_____

_____

D. Explaining Processes or Demonstrating

_____

_____

E. Exposition

_____

_____

III. Criteria for Evaluating Informative Speeches

_____

_____

_____

_____

Key Terms

intellectually stimulating (p. 429)

_____

_____

creativity (p. 430)

_____

_____

relevance (p. 433)

_____

_____

vital information (p. 433)

_____

_____

mnemonics (p. 436)

_____

_____

acronyms (p. 436)

_____

_____

association (p. 436)

_____

_____

narrative (p. 437)

_____

_____

describing (p. 438)

_____

_____

defining (p. 440)

_____

_____

synonyms (p. 44)

_____

_____

antonyms (p. 44)

_____

_____

etymology (p. 440)

_____

_____

explaining processes (p. 441)

_____

_____

284

complete demonstration (p. 442)

_____

_____

modified demonstration (p. 442)

_____

_____

expository speech (p. 443)

_____

_____

Exercises
Journal Activities

📖 Journal Activity 17.1 – Different Ways of Presenting Information (p. 443)
Evaluate the two different ways of presenting variable temperature data suggested in the text on page 433. Indicate which way you believe is better and explain why. Next, create a third way which is different. Is the way you created even better? If so, explain why. If not, explain why not.

<u>17.2 Using InfoTrac College Edition (p. 428)</u>
Using InfoTrac College Edition, under the subject of "learning," click on "Learning, Psychology of." Look for articles that discuss "how people learn" and "how people think" to gain additional information that is relevant to informative speaking. Read one or more articles to help you better understand how to prepare your informative speech. Summarize your findings below.

17.3 Using InfoTrac College Edition

The use of mnemonics and acronyms can enhance your informative speaking skills. How? Using InfoTrac College Edition, type in "mnemonic" as your key word. Find and read the article "ART: acronyms reinforce training" by Diane Ullius. Answer the following questions:

1. According to Ullius, what are two advantages to using mnemonics in public speaking?

2. What are three rules for using acronyms in a speech?

3. For your informative speech, identify any material that could be emphasized by use of an acronym. What is the acronym? Describe how you can use it in the speech.

17.4 Using Technology (p. 437)

Informative speeches become more interesting when the information seems relevant and the speaker credible. One way to enhance your credibility and to acquire information that is specific to your speech is to correspond through e-mail with a respected expert on the subject. In your e-mail message to an expert, ask a specific question that is relevant to your topic and not answered in the existing printed material you have found. Then you can report the answers you receive in your speech as follows: "In an e-mail I received from… she told me that…"

Name of person to E-Mail: _____

E-Mail Address: _____

Question & Response:

17.5 Using Technology

Adding humor to a speech is one way to add emphasis to a point and interest to the speech in general. Visit http://www.public-speaking.org/public-speaking-articles.htm#humor or a similar web site that offers humorous quotations, anecdotes, and stories. See if you can find a way to add humor to at least one point in your speech. Summarize your efforts in the space below. Be sure to record any necessary bibliographic information so that you may cite your source in the speech.

17.6 Informative Speech Self-Critique

Use the checklist on the page that follows to critique an informative speech. You may choose to critique the videotaped speech rehearsal you made in exercise 16.6, a newer version of that speech that incorporates changes made as a result of exercise 16.6, the speech titled "Black Box" on your Communicate! CD-ROM, another speech on video, or a speech your instructor provides. (Save the other 2 speeches on the Communicate! CD-ROM for later exercises.)

INFORMATIVE SPEECH CRITIQUE SHEET

Name of Speaker: _____

Title/Topic of Speech: _____

Mark each item on a scale of 1-5:
(5 = excellent, 4 = good, 3 = satisfactory, 2 = fair, 1 = poor.)

Primary Criteria:

_____ 1. Was the specific goal designed to increase audience information?
_____ 2. Did the speaker show creativity in idea development?
_____ 3. Was the speaker effective in establishing his/her credibility?
_____ 4. Was the information intellectually stimulating?
_____ 5. Did the speaker show the relevance of the information?
_____ 6. Did the speaker emphasize the information?
_____ 7. Was the organizational pattern appropriate for the intent and content of the
           speech?

General Criteria:

_____ 1. Was the specific goal clear?
_____ 2. Was the introduction effective?
_____ 3. Were the main points clear?
_____ 4. Was the conclusion effective?
_____ 5. Was the language clear, vivid and emphatic?
_____ 6. Was the speech delivered enthusiastically, with vocal expressiveness,
           spontaneously, fluently, and with eye contact?

Comments:

Based on these criteria, evaluate the speech as (check one):

_____ excellent, _____ good, _____ satisfactory, _____ fair, _____ poor.

<u>17.7 Speech Adaptation Plan</u>
Using the sample on page 447 as a guide, develop a plan for adapting your informative speech to your audience. Refer to earlier exercises from previous chapters and the text as needed.

1. Getting and maintaining interest:

2. Facilitating understanding:

3. Increasing retention:

17.8 What Would You Do? (p. 451)
Read the *What Would You Do: A Question of Ethics* scenario on page 451 of your text. Answer the following questions in the space provided here.

1. Is Paul's proposed behavior unethical? Why?

2. What should Gina say to challenge Paul's last statement?

17.9 Using the Communicate! CD-ROM (p. 445-451)
Click on "Speech Interactive," and then "Shakespeare." Watch the speech and then answer the questions in the "Evaluation" section. When finished, click on the "Done" button to compare your answers to those of the authors. How did the two sets of answers compare?
(Note: An outline, speech plan and speech transcript for this speech appear in your text on pages 445-451.)

17.10 Using the Communicate! CD-ROM (p. 445-451)
Continuing with the "Shakespeare" speech evaluated in exercise 17.9, click on "Critique" and critique the speech on the five areas addressed on the CD-ROM. Guidelines for critiquing informative speeches appear in the link "guidelines" and in Chapter 17 of your text. When you are finished, click on the "Done" button to compare your criticisms with those of the authors of the text. How do your answers compare?
(Note: An outline, speech plan and speech transcript for this speech appear in your text on pages 445-451.)

Chapter 17 Quiz Questions (answers and page references in Appendix)

True/False

1. "A story, tale, or account that has a point or climax" is the definition of a narrative.

2. Since repetition of key ideas is boring, it cannot be an effective form of emphasis.

3. "The hail stone was about the size of a baseball, and twice as heavy" is an example of description.

4. "Antonyms" are words that have the same or nearly the same meanings.

5. It is possible for an entire main point, or even an entire speech, to be an extended definition.

Multiple Choice

1. One of the reasons for citing your sources (showing you "did your homework") is to:
   a. show creativity
   b. provide emphasis
   c. enhance credibility
   d. show relevance

2. Sara is giving her speech on tobacco production. After she gives a statistic on how much tobacco is harvested each year in this country, she repeats the statistic, pauses briefly, smiles, and says "That's *a lot* of smoke!" Sara is trying to
   a. substitute for a visual aid
   b. enhance credibility
   c. add emphasis
   d. show relevance

3. The letters "NCAA" are one example of a(n)
   a. acronym
   b. synonym
   c. antonym
   d. definition
   e. word association

4. Stuart gives his speech on "How to make chocolate chip cookies." His speech is most likely to be
   a. an extended example
   b. a demonstration or process explanation
   c. an extended definition
   d. an exposition

5. "The causes for criminal behavior" is most likely a topic for
    a. demonstrative speaking
    b. extemporaneous speaking
    c. definitional speaking
    d. expository speaking

Essay

1. List and describe each of the methods of informing discussed in the text. Include an example of each.

2. Describe how you might organize an informative speech on how to do some simple process (such as a recipe). What method if informing would this be?

Useful and Interesting Internet Links

http://www.demon.co.uk/mindtool/memory.html - A site for learning more about mnemonics and other skills used to improve memory.

http://dir.yahoo.com/Social_Science/Linguisitics_and_Human_Languages/Etymology/ - This site allows you to research word origins.

http://www.webcorp.com/sounds/nixon.htm - Audio archives of historical figures. Some excellent speech segments.

http://www.public-speaking.org/public-speaking-articles.htm#humor - A list of links for tips, techniques and samples for using humor in speeches.

http://www.historychannel.com/speeches/index.html - An archive of great speeches presented by *The History Channel*.

http://www.cs.queensu.ca/FAQs/email/websrch.html - An online resource for finding individual's e-mail addresses.

CHAPTER 18: Persuasive Speaking

Learning Objectives

After studying this chapter, you should be able to answer the following questions:

- What is the difference between affecting behavior and moving to action?
- What is the value of assessing audience attitude toward the goal?
- What are good reasons?
- What kinds of materials give support to reasons?
- What are some common fallacies?
- What are typical persuasive speaking organizational patterns?
- What does a persuasive speaker do to motivate an audience?
- What are major ethical guidelines?

Interactive Chapter Outline

I. Principles of Persuasive Speaking

_____

_____

   A. Writing a Specific Goal

_____

_____

   B. Adapting to Audience Attitude

_____

_____

_____

_____

   C. Giving Good Reasons and Evidence

_____

_____

_____

_____

_____

_____

D. Organizing Reasons to Meet Audience Attitudes

_____

_____

_____

_____

E. Motivation

_____

_____

_____

_____

F. Building Credibility

_____

_____

G. Gender and Cultural Differences

_____

_____

H. Presentation

_____

_____

II. Criteria for Evaluating Persuasive Speeches

_____

_____

_____

_____

Key Terms

persuasive speaking (p. 456)

_____

_____

attitude (p. 457)

_____

_____

opinion (p. 457)

_____

_____

reasons (p. 460)

_____

_____

reasoning by generalization from example (p. 464)

_____

_____

reasoning by causation (p. 465)

_____

_____

reasoning by analogy (p. 465)

_____

_____

296

reasoning by sign (p. 466)

_____

_____

hasty generalization (p. 466)

_____

_____

false cause (p. 466)

_____

_____

appeal to authority (p. 467)

_____

_____

ad hominem argument (p. 467)

_____

_____

motivation (p. 470)

_____

_____

incentive (p. 470)

_____

_____

emotions (p. 472)

_____

_____

Exercises
Journal Activities

📖 <u>Journal Activity 18.1 – Writing Persuasive Speech Goals (p. 457)</u>
In the space provided below, write the specific goal you are considering for your persuasive speech assignment, and then rewrite it two or three times with slightly different wordings.
Identify your goal as one establishing or changing a belief or as one seeking action. If at this stage you do not know what your audience believes, you may wish to hold off on the final wording of your goal until you finish Journal Activity 18.2.

📖 Journal Activity 18.2 – Assessing Audience Attitudes (p. 460)

In the space provided below, answer the following questions:

In reference to your specific persuasive speech goal, is your audience's attitude likely to be in favor, neutral, or opposed?

What speech strategies will you use to adapt to that attitude?

📖 Journal Activity 18.3 – Selecting Reasons (p. 466)

In the space provided below, write the specific goal you will use for your first persuasive speech.

1. Write at least six reasons that support your specific goal.

2. Place stars next to the three or four reasons you are planning to use. Briefly explain why they are the best.

Journal Activity 18.4 – Selecting an Organization (p. 470)

Select a pattern of organization for your persuasive speech. In the space below, discuss why you are planning to use this organization. Answer why you think it fits in well with what you believe will be your audience's reaction to your goal.

18.5 Outlining Persuasive Speeches

Develop an outline for your persuasive speech. Use the persuasive speech organization and outlining templates found in the "Useful and Interesting Internet Links" section of this chapter, or use the forms provided at the end of the chapter.

18.6 Using InfoTrac College Edition (p. 464)

Under the subject "attitude change," click on "Periodical references." Look for articles that discuss how audiences process information. Make a special effort to find an article or articles by Richard Petty. Summarize your findings here.

18.7 Using InfoTrac College Edition

Using "persuasion techniques" as your search term, locate the article "Get your way using lawyers' techniques" by Noelle C. Nelson. Summarize the techniques the article presents and how you may use them in your speech, focusing on the following:

1. How does Nelson's argument about the failure of the prosecutors in the O. J. Simpson trial "to clearly and explicitly ask for what they wanted" fit in with Monroe's motivational pattern?

2. Draft a statement where you clearly and explicitly ask for what you want in your first persuasive speech.

3. How is Nelson's advice to use "everyday language" consistent with the motivational pattern of speech organization?

18.8 Using Technology (p. 474)
Who better to demonstrate persuasive speaking skills but a lawyer? Watch *The Practice, Law & Order, Family Law*, or some other show that depicts a legal trial. Evaluate the way the attorneys try to persuade the jury to accept their point of view. What do they do to build their credibility? How do they incorporate emotional appeal in their remarks? How do they reason with juries? What do they do that makes them particularly effective or ineffective in their speeches? Summarize your findings here.

<u>18.9 What Would You Do? (p. 484)</u>
Read the *What Would You Do: A Question of Ethics* scenario on page 484 of your text. Answer the following questions in the space provided here.

1. Would it be ethical for Alejandro to give his speech in this way? If so, why?

2. If not, what would he need to do to make the speech ethical?

<u>18.10 Using the Communicate! CD-ROM (p. 479-483)</u>
Click on "Speech Interactive," and then "Trucks." Watch the speech and then answer the questions in the "Evaluation" section. When finished, click on the "Done" button to compare your answers to those of the authors. How did the two sets of answers compare?

Continuing with the "Trucks" speech, click on "Critique" and critique the speech on the seven areas addressed on the CD-ROM. Guidelines for critiquing informative speeches appear in the link "guidelines" and in Chapter 18 of your text. When you are finished, click on the "Done" button to compare your criticisms with those of the authors of the text. How do your answers compare?
(<u>Note</u>: An outline, speech plan and speech transcript for this speech appear in your text on pages 479-483.)

<u>18.11 Persuasive Speech Self-Critique</u>
Use the checklist on the page that follows to critique a persuasive speech. You may choose to critique a videotaped version of your own persuasive speech, the speech titled "Trucks" on your Communicate! CD-ROM, another speech on video, or a speech your instructor provides.

PERSUASIVE SPEECH CRITIQUE SHEET

Name of Speaker: _____

Title/Topic of Speech: _____

Mark each item on a scale of 1-5:
(5 = excellent, 4 = good, 3 = satisfactory, 2 = fair, 1 = poor.)

Primary Criteria:

_____ 1. Was the specific goal designed to affect a belief or move the audience to action?
_____ 2. Did the speaker present clearly stated reasons?
_____ 3. Did the speaker use facts and expert opinions to support these reasons?
_____ 4. Was the organizational pattern appropriate for the type of goal and assumed attitude of the audience?
_____ 5. Did the speaker use emotional language to motivate the audience?
_____ 6. Was the speaker effective in establishing his/her credibility on this topic?
_____ 7. Was the speaker ethical in handling material?

General Criteria:

_____ 1. Was the specific goal clear?
_____ 2. Was the introduction effective?
_____ 3. Was the organizational pattern appropriate for the intent and content of the speech?
_____ 4. Was the conclusion effective?
_____ 5. Was the language clear, vivid and emphatic and appropriate?
_____ 6. Was the delivery convincing?

Comments:

Based on these criteria, evaluate the speech as (check one):

_____ excellent, _____ good, _____ satisfactory, _____ fair, _____ poor.

Chapter 18 Quiz Questions (answers and page references in Appendix)

True/False

1. "Reasons" and "evidence" is the same thing.

2. If an audience is highly in favor of your speech goal, then you should emphasize motivation and practical suggestions.

3. The three tests of good evidence are: reliable source, recent, and relevant.

4. Reasoning by sign is considered the weakest type of reasoning.

5. The comparative advantages format focuses on the cause of the problem.

Multiple Choice

1. Pierre is giving a persuasive speech on why we should stiffen penalties for drinking and driving. He wants to present three reasons why we should do this. His speech is likely to be organized using
   - a. problem-solution order
   - b. logical reasons order
   - c. motivated sequence order
   - d. comparative advantages order

2. Leticia argues we should not do what George suggests because "George is an idiot!" This is an example of
   - a. an ad hominem argument
   - b. a logical reasons argument
   - c. a motivational appeal
   - d. an appeal to authority
   - e. an appeal to credibility

3. Acceptance into the group is an example of
   - a. a physiological need
   - b. a cognitive need
   - c. a safety need
   - d. a belongingness and love need

4. Which of the following is NOT a way to build credibility with your audience?
   - a. resist personal attacks
   - b. give sources for all information
   - c. tell the truth
   - d. use a hasty generalization
   - e. all are acceptable for building credibility

5. Carol is giving her persuasive speech. She is dressed well, articulate, clear, makes eye contact, and looks relaxed and confident. Carol probably realizes that
- a. an audience can be deceived by ad hominem delivery
- b. delivery matters little in persuasive speaking
- c. you are more likely to persuade an audience if you have an effective oral presentation style.
- d. arousing emotions is not very useful

Essay

1. Discuss several things a speaker must do to build credibility when preparing and giving a persuasive speech.

2. Why is it important to have good reasons to support your speech goal? What is the relationship between reasons and evidence?

Useful and Interesting Internet Links

http://www.vscc.cc.tn.us/dew/103perlogicalreasons.htm - Outlining and organization form for a persuasive speech in Logical Reasons order.

http://www.vscc.cc.tn.us/dew/103perproblemsolution.htm - Outlining and organization form for a persuasive speech in Problem-Solution order.

http://www.vscc.cc.tn.us/dew/103peradvantag.htm - Outlining and organization form for a persuasive speech in Comparative Advantage order.

http://www.vscc.cc.tn.us/dew/103permotivate.htm - Outlining and organization form for a persuasive speech using a motivational pattern.

http://www.ukans.edu/cwis/units/coms2/vpa/vpa5.htm - How to support your points from the Virtual Presentation Assistant at the University of Kansas.

http://www.influenceatwork.com/indexacademic.html - "Influence at Work: The Psychology of Persuasion" offers theoretical discussions and practical examples of how persuasion influences us.

http://chuma.cas.usf.edu/~mivusic/bhrt1.html - An interesting site that uses scenes from the movie *Braveheart* as the basis for teaching how to analyze persuasive appeals.

http://chiron.valdosta.edu/whuitt/col/regsys/maslow.html- More detailed information on Maslow and his hierarchy of needs.

Organization and Outline Forms for Persuasive Speeches

Statement of Logical Reasons

Title:_____

Specific Goal:_____

INTRODUCTION

I. _____

_____

_____

II. _____

_____

Thesis Statement: _____

_____

BODY

I. Main point (the problem is...)_____

  A. Major point (history of the problem)_____

    1. Subpoint (the problem started when...)_____

      a. Support (a statistic, narrative, example, definition, testimony, or comparison)_____

      b. Support (a statistic, narrative, example, definition, testimony, or comparison)_____

    2. Subpoint (the problem started because...)_____

      a. Support (a statistic, narrative, example, definition, testimony, or comparison)_____

      b. Support (a statistic, narrative, example, definition,

testimony, or comparison)_____

   3. Subpoint (the problem is extensive)_____

      a. Support (a statistic, narrative, example, definition, testimony, or comparison)_____

      b. Support (a statistic, narrative, example, definition, testimony, or comparison)_____

B. Major point (the problem is harmful)_____

   1. Subpoint (the specific harms are several)_____

      a. Subpoint (harm 1 is...)_____

      b. Subpoint (harm 2 is...)_____

      c. Subpoint (harm 3 is...)_____

   2. Subpoint (the harms will continue or increase unless we make a change)_____

      a. Support (a statistic, narrative, example, definition, testimony, or comparison)_____

      b. Support (a statistic, narrative, example, definition, testimony, or comparison)_____

Transition to second main point

_____

II. Main point (the solution is...)_____

  A. Major point (the solution will solve the problem)_____

    1. Subpoint (it is practical)_____

       a. Support (a statistic, narrative, example, definition, testimony, or comparison)_____

       b. Support (a statistic, narrative, example, definition, testimony, or comparison)_____

    2. Subpoint (it is feasible)_____

    a. Support (a statistic, narrative, example, definition, testimony, or comparison)_____

    b. Support (a statistic, narrative, example, definition, testimony, or comparison)_____

B. Major point (the solution can be accomplished)_____

  1. Subpoint (the plan is to proceed this way)_____

    a. Step 1 is:_____

    b. Step 2 is:_____

    c. Step 3 is:_____

  2. Subpoint (who will put the plan into operation)_____

    a. Subpoint (their competence is known)_____

      (1) Support _____

      (2) Support _____

    b. Subpoint (audience members must do this...)_____

      _____

CONCLUSION

I. _____

_____

II. _____

_____

SOURCES

Problem-Solution

Title:_____

Specific Goal:_____

INTRODUCTION

I. _____

_____

_____

II. _____

_____

Attention-getting material:_____

_____

Material to relate subject to audience lives:_____

_____

Preview of the speech:_____

_____

Thesis Statement: _____

_____

BODY

I. Main point (state the problem)_____

_____

  A. Major point (problem description)_____

_____

    1. Subpoint (one effect of the problem)_____

_____

    a. Support (a statistic, narrative, example, definition, testimony, or comparison)_____

    b. Support (a statistic, narrative, example, definition, testimony, or comparison)_____

  2. Subpoint (another effect of the problem)_____

    a. Support (a statistic, narrative, example, definition, testimony, or comparison)_____

    b. Support (a statistic, narrative, example, definition, testimony, or comparison)_____

B. Major point (problem is important because)_____

_____

  1. Subpoint (problem is extensive)_____

_____

    a. Support (a statistic, narrative, example, definition, testimony, or comparison)_____

    b. Support (a statistic, narrative, example, definition, testimony, or comparison)_____

  2. Subpoint (Who is affected)_____

_____

    a. Support (a statistic, narrative, example, definition, testimony, or comparison)_____

    b. Support (a statistic, narrative, example, definition, testimony, or comparison)_____

C. Major point (problem has consequences that will continue)

_____

  1. Subpoint to explain Major point_____

    a. Support (a statistic, narrative, example, definition, testimony, or comparison)_____

    b. Support (a statistic, narrative, example, definition, testimony, or comparison)_____

  2. Subpoint to explain Major point_____

    a. Support (a statistic, narrative, example, definition, testimony, or comparison)_____

    b. Support (a statistic, narrative, example, definition, testimony, or comparison)_____
        Transition to second main point

_____

II. Main point (state the solution)_____

_____

  A. Major point (describe the solution)_____

_____

    1. Subpoint (solution fits the problem because)_____

_____

      a. Subpoint (addresses the causes because)_____

_____

        Example: Support (a statistic, narrative, example, definition, testimony, or comparison)

_____

      b. Subpoint (will work because)_____

_____

        Example: Support (a statistic, narrative, example, definition, testimony, or comparison)

_____

   2. Subpoint (can be implemented because)_____

          _____

       a. Support (a statistic, narrative, example, definition, testimony, or comparison)_____

       b. Support (a statistic, narrative, example, definition, testimony, or comparison)_____

   3. Subpoint (the plan has steps)_____

       a. Step 1 is:_____

       b. Step 2 is:_____

    4. Subpoint (the plan requires)_____

       a. Finance and/or time(?)_____

       b. Personnel and/or effort (?)_____

B. Major point (visualize the results)_____

   1. Subpoint (the results we expect are)_____

       a. Support (a statistic, narrative, example, definition, testimony, or comparison)_____

       b. Support (a statistic, narrative, example, definition, testimony, or comparison)_____

   2. Subpoint (additional positive results are)_____

       a. Support (a statistic, narrative, example, definition, testimony, or comparison)_____

       b. Support (a statistic, narrative, example, definition, testimony, or comparison)_____

   3.Subpoint (results should occur by this time)_____

       a. Support (a statistic, narrative, example, definition, testimony, or comparison)_____

       b. Support (a statistic, narrative, example, definition,

testimony, or comparison)_____

CONCLUSION

I. _____

_____

II. _____

_____

Summary of main ideas_____

_____

Concluding remarks:_____

_____

SOURCES

Comparative Advantages

Title: _____

Specific Goal: _____

INTRODUCTION

I. _____

_____

_____

II. _____

_____

Attention-getting material:_____

_____

Material to relate subject to audience lives:_____

_____

Preview of the speech:_____

_____

Thesis Statement: _____

_____

BODY

I. Main point (solution 1)_____

  A. Major point (strengths)_____
    1. Subpoint (strength #1 is...)_____

      a. Support (a statistic, narrative, example, definition, testimony, or comparison)_____

      b. Support (a statistic, narrative, example, definition, testimony, or comparison)_____

2. Subpoint (strength #2 is...)_____

   a. Support (a statistic, narrative, example, definition, testimony, or comparison)_____

   b. Support (a statistic, narrative, example, definition, testimony, or comparison)_____

B. Major point (weaknesses)_____

  1. Subpoint (weakness #1 is...)_____

   a. Support (a statistic, narrative, example, definition, testimony, or comparison)_____

   b. Support (a statistic, narrative, example, definition, testimony, or comparison)_____

  2. Subpoint (weakness #1 is...)_____

   a. Support (a statistic, narrative, example, definition, testimony, or comparison)_____

   b. Support (a statistic, narrative, example, definition, testimony, or comparison)_____

Transition to second main point

_____

II. Main point (solution 2)_____

A. Major point (strengths)_____

  1. Subpoint (strength #1 is...)_____

   a. Support (a statistic, narrative, example, definition, testimony, or comparison)_____

   b. Support (a statistic, narrative, example, definition, testimony, or comparison)_____

  2. Subpoint (strength #2 is...)_____

        a. Support (a statistic, narrative, example, definition, testimony, or comparison)_____

        b. Support (a statistic, narrative, example, definition, testimony, or comparison)_____

  B. Major point (weaknesses)_____

    1. Subpoint (weakness #1 is...)_____

        a. Support (a statistic, narrative, example, definition, testimony, or comparison)_____

        b. Support (a statistic, narrative, example, definition, testimony, or comparison)_____

    2. Subpoint (weakness #1 is...)_____

        a. Support (a statistic, narrative, example, definition, testimony, or comparison)_____

        b. Support (a statistic, narrative, example, definition, testimony, or comparison)_____

        Transition to third main point

_____

III. Main point (solution 3)_____

  A. Major point (strengths)_____

    1. Subpoint (strength #1 is...)_____

        a. Support (a statistic, narrative, example, definition, testimony, or comparison)_____

        b. Support (a statistic, narrative, example, definition, testimony, or comparison)_____

    2. Subpoint (strength #2 is...)_____

        a. Support (a statistic, narrative, example, definition, testimony, or comparison)_____

        b. Support (a statistic, narrative, example, definition,

testimony, or comparison)_____

3. Conclusion (solution #3 has more or worthwhile advantages than #1 or #2 because...)_____

    a._____

    b._____

    c._____

B. Major point (weaknesses)_____

  1. Subpoint (weakness #1 is...)_____

    a. Support (a statistic, narrative, example, definition, testimony, or comparison)_____

    b. Support (a statistic, narrative, example, definition, testimony, or comparison)_____

  2. Subpoint (weakness #1 is...)_____

    a. Support (a statistic, narrative, example, definition, testimony, or comparison)_____

    b. Support (a statistic, narrative, example, definition, testimony, or comparison)_____

  3. Conclusion (solution #3 has fewer disadvantages or less significant disadvantages than solution #1 or #2 because...)_____

    a._____

    b._____

    c._____

CONCLUSION

I. _____

_____

318

II. _____

_____

Summary of Solution #3 minimal weaknesses and superior
strengths_____

_____

Concluding remarks:_____

_____

SOURCES

Motivated Sequence

Title:_____

Specific Goal:_____

INTRODUCTION

I. _____

_____

_____

II. _____

_____

ATTENTION-getting material:_____

_____   _____

Material to relate problem to audience lives:_____

_____

Preview of the speech:_____

_____

Thesis Statement: _____

_____

BODY

I. Main point (state the NEED FOR ACTION)_____

_____

   A. Major point (problem description)_____

_____

1. Subpoint (one effect of the problem)_____

    _____

    a. Support (a statistic, narrative, example, definition, testimony, or comparison)_____

    b. Support (a statistic, narrative, example, definition, testimony, or comparison)_____

2. Subpoint (another effect of the problem)_____

    a. Support (a statistic, narrative, example, definition, testimony, or comparison)_____

    b. Support (a statistic, narrative, example, definition, testimony, or comparison)_____

B. Major point (problem is important because)_____

    _____

    1. Subpoint (problem is extensive)_____

        _____

        a. Support (a statistic, narrative, example, definition, testimony, or comparison)_____

        b. Support (a statistic, narrative, example, definition, testimony, or comparison)_____

    2. Subpoint (Who is affected)_____

        _____

        a. Support (a statistic, narrative, example, definition, testimony, or comparison)_____

        b. Support (a statistic, narrative, example, definition, testimony, or comparison)_____

C. Major point (problem has consequences that will continue)

    _____

    1. Subpoint to explain why_____

  a. Support (a statistic, narrative, example, definition, testimony, or comparison)_____

  b. Support (a statistic, narrative, example, definition, testimony, or comparison)_____

 2. Subpoint to explain why_____

  a. Support (a statistic, narrative, example, definition, testimony, or comparison)_____

  b. Support (a statistic, narrative, example, definition, testimony, or comparison)_____

   Transition to second main point

_____

II. Main point (state the solution to SATISFY the need)_____

_____

 A. Major point (describe the solution)_____

  1. Step #1 is_____

  2. Step #2 is_____

  3. Step #3 is_____

 B. Major point (solution satisfies the need because...)

  1. Support (a statistic, narrative, example, definition, testimony, or comparison)_____

  2. Support (a statistic, narrative, example, definition, testimony, or comparison)_____

 C. Major point (solution can be implemented because)_____

_____

  1. Support (a statistic, narrative, example, definition, testimony, or comparison)_____

    2. Support (a statistic, narrative, example, definition, testimony, or comparison)_____

III. Main point (VISUALIZE the results)_____

    A. Major point (the results we expect will be...)_____

        1. Support (a statistic, narrative, example, definition, testimony, or comparison)_____

        2. Support (a statistic, narrative, example, definition, testimony, or comparison)_____

    B. Major point (the consequences of not acting will be...)_____

_____

        1. Support (a statistic, narrative, example, definition, testimony, or comparison)_____

        2. Support (a statistic, narrative, example, definition, testimony, or comparison)_____

CONCLUSION

I. _____

_____

II. _____

_____

Summary of main ideas_____

_____

Concluding remarks (a specific call for the audience to take ACTION)_____

_____

SOURCES

Answers to sample true/false and multiple choice quiz questions

(Page numbers refer to pages in textbook where the concept in question is discussed.)

PART I

<u>Chapter 1:</u>
T/F
1. T (p. 8)
2. F (p. 8)
3. F (p. 9)
4. F (p. 21)
5. T (p. 12)

M/C
1. C (p. 17)
2. A (p. 6)
3. B (p. 7)
4. D (p. 9)
5. C (p. 20)

<u>Chapter 2:</u>
T/F
1. T (p. 30)
2. T (p. 35)
3. F (p. 30)
4. F (p. 32)
5. T (p. 45)

M/C
1. A (p. 32)
2. C (p. 31)
3. D (p. 34)
4. B (p. 35)
5. A (p. 43)

<u>Chapter 3:</u>
T/F
1. T (p. 52)
2. T (p. 53)
3. T (p. 53)
4. F (p. 56)
5. T (p. 61)

M/C
1. B (p. 53)
2. C (p. 67)

3. E (p. 61)
4. C (p. 61)
5. A (p. 65)

<u>Chapter 4:</u>
T/F
1. F (p. 91)
2. T (p. 78)
3. F (p. 84)
4. T (p. 87)
5. T (p. 76)

M/C
1. D (p. 80)
2. C (p. 77)
3. B (p. 77)
4. C (p. 79)
5. A (p. 78)

PART II

<u>Chapter 5:</u>
T/F
1. F (p. 112)
2. F (p. 114)
3. F (p. 115)
4. T (p. 103)
5. T (p. 102)

M/C
1. B (p. 99)
2. C (p.108)
3. A (p. 110)
4. D (p. 110)
5. E (p. 102)

<u>Chapter 6:</u>
T/F
1. T (p. 130)
2. F (p. 126)
3. F (p. 135)
4. F (p. 137)
5. T (p. 140)

M/C
1. A (p. 126)
2. C (p. 126)
3. B (p. 128)
4. D (p. 130)
5. B (p. 135)

Chapter 7:
T/F
1. T (p. 172)
2. T (p. 172)
3. T (p. 157)
4. F (p. 170)
5. T (p. 159)

M/C
1. B (p. 156)
2. C (p. 156)
3. E (p. 171)
4. C (p. 174-175)
5. A (p. 172)

Chapter 8:
T/F
1. F (p. 202)
2. T (p. 202-204)
3. T (p. 188-190)
4. F (p. 190)
5. F (p. 206-207)

M/C
1. B (p. 187)
2. A (p. 200)
3. C (p. 199)
4. D (p. 203)
5. B (p. 198)

Chapter 9:
T/F
1. F (p. 222)
2. T (p. 227)
3. F (p. 227)
4. T (p. 229)
5. T (p. 230)

M/C
1. C (p. 220-221)
2. D (p. 230)
3. A (p. 228)
4. E (p. 226)
5. C (p. 226)

PART III
Chapter 10:
T/F
1. T (p. 240)
2. F (p. 256-257)
3. T (p. 255)
4. F (p. 244)
5. F (p. 238)

M/C
1. A (p. 255)
2. B (p. 251)
3. D (p. 243)
4. B (p. 248)
5. A (p. 250)

Chapter 11:
T/F
1. T (p. 268)
2. F (p. 268)
3. F (p. 272)
4. F (p. 277)
5. T (p. 271)

M/C
1. D (p. 283)
2. A (p. 264)
3. C (p. 265)
4. B (p. 271)
5. B (p. 271)

Part IV
Chapter 12:
T/F
1. F (p. 301)
2. F (p. 290)
3. T (p. 294)
4. T (p. 296)
5. T (p. 298)

M/C
1. A (p. 291)
2. C (p. 302)
3. D (p. 296)
4. D (p. 294)
5. B (p. 296)

Chapter 13:
T/F
1. F (p. 326)
2. T (p. 320)
3. F (p. 323)
4. F (p. 314)
5. T (p. 308)

M/C
1. D (p. 308)
2. C (p. 308-309)
3. D (p. 311)
4. C (p. 315)
5. A (p. 319)

Chapter 14:
T/F
1. F (p. 346)
2. T (p. 341)
3. T (p. 338)
4. F (p. 348)
5. T (p. 351)

M/C
1. A (p. 336)
2. E (p. 338)
3. D (p. 341
4. C (p. 345)
5. B (p. 348)

Chapter 15:
T/F
1. F (p. 386)
2. F (p. 380)
3. T (p. 384)
4. F (p. 367)
5. F (p. 372)

M/C
1. C (p. 375)
2. A (p. 363)
3. B (p. 370)
4. D (p. 379)
5. A (p. 378)

Chapter 16:
T/F
1. F (p. 410)
2. F (p. 394)
3. T (p. 401)
4. F (p. 406)
5. T (p. 408)

M/C
1. B (p. 395)
2. A (p. 397)
3. D (p. 402)
4. C (p. 406)
5. A (p. 417)

Chapter 17:
T/F
1. T (p. 437)
2. F (p. 434)
3. T (p. 438)
4. F (p. 440)
5. T (p. 441)

M/C
1. C (p. 428)
2. C (p. 435)
3. A (p. 436)
4. B (p. 441)
5. D (p. 443)

Chapter 18:
T/F
1. F (p. 460)
2. T (p. 461)
3. T (p. 464)
4. F (p. 465)
5. F (p. 468)

M/C
1. B (p. 467)
2. A (p. 467)
3. D (p. 471)
4. D (p. 474-475)
5. C (p. 477)

The Crew of Alaska Air 261 struggled desperately to correct a problem with the aircraft's horizontal stabilizers. But by the time they realized the true scope of the problem, it was too late; and the aircraft spiraled into the Pacific Ocean, killing all 88 people onboard. But how do we know this? Certainly not from any eyewitness accounts--everybody onboard the flight perished. The source of this information according to *Newsweek,* February 14, 1999, is a device of which most people have heard, but of which very few know very much. The source of this information is none other than the black box.

CNN, April 15, 1999, tells us that the black box has been responsible in literally thousands of air crashes—both in discovering their cause as well as in determining what must be done in the future so that the same failure is not repeated. My purpose today is to first explain some features and functions of the black box; second, to explore it's current status, and third, to elucidate some of the new and upcoming developments stemming from its technology.

First of all, let's look at the black box features and functions. To begin with, CNN, September 9, 1991, tells us that the name itself is a misnomer. The elusive black box isn't even black, nor is it a single box. It's actually made up of two separate units painted bright orange to facilitate easier recovery in the field. These two units are known as the flight data recorder and the cockpit voice recorder. The web page of the National Transportation Safety Bureau, dated December 20,1999, tells us that the flight data recorder can monitor up to several hundred aspects of an aircraft's performance and can do so for up to 25 hours straight.

The cockpit voice recorder on the other hand, monitors in a 30-minute continuous tape loop and is made up of several different tape recorders: one in the headset of each crew member on a given aircraft and one suspended in the cockpit, which allows it to pick up noises both from the cockpit area as well as from other parts of the aircraft noises which can be vital in discovering the cause of a crash. Both the flight data recorder and the cockpit voice recorder have a heat resistance of up to 2000 degrees Fahrenheit for up to half an hour and a water resistance of up to 20,000 feet deep. It has a locator beacon which guides investigators to the crash site even if it's underwater, and an impact tolerance of up to 3400 times the force of gravity or 3400 Gs, a force by which only humans can only withstand about one quarter of one percent. According to ABC News June 22, 1999, some of the harsh tests that this device endures include dropping a 500-pound weight on the device from a height of 10 feet and shooting it out of a pneumatic cannon at 300 miles per hour into a wall just 18 inches away. The devices which survive these harsh tests are then installed on our aircraft.

So now that we've looked at how the box gets onto the aircraft in the first place, let's look at the job it's done since it has gotten there.

Aviation Week, December 6, 1999, tells us that one example of how a black box can be used in a preliminary investigation can be seen in the current, ongoing investigation in to the crash of the Egypt Air 990. Now the flight data recorder shows that the only possible mechanical failure which could explain the crash would have had to come from the electric system. However, the cockpit voice recorder shows something more chilling. The cockpit voice recorder leaves no room open for mechanical failure and leaves only two possible alternatives for the crash. The crash was due either to pilot error, or was a direct attempted suicide on the part of one of the co-pilots.

However, not only can a black box be used in a preliminary investigation, *Aviation Week,* March 22, 1999, tells us that they can also be hooked up to a simulator, placing the investigators themselves in the pilot's seat and recreating every single circumstance of the individual crash—making the solution that much easier to find. Unfortunately, even this amazing device has its flaws.

The largest of these flaws according to *Aviation Week,* September 21, 1999, is the fact that the black box depends on the aircraft itself for power. Thus, when the aircraft in the midst of a crisis situation loses power, the recorders simply stop recording, leaving the last several minutes of the crash a big question mark. And according to ABC News September 26, 1999, this has happened in a total of 52 air accidents since 1983, when the latest model of the black box was installed.

These air accidents include Egypt Air 990; including as well as the highly publicized crash of TWA 800 back in 1996. This problem will be remedied shortly however, according to the Federal Aviation Administration. In June 1999, all new black boxes must be produced with an independent ten-minute backup power supply. Once these new black boxes are installed, this will make the black box's life-saving function that much more effective.

Interestingly enough though, this device which we think of as exclusive to the airline industries has already shown itself very effective in others areas as well. One such area can be seen in the *New York Daily News,* March 17, 1999, in a crash between an Amtrak passenger train and a big rig, which killed 11 and injured over 100 more. Black boxes were pulled from both vehicles and showed that neither had malfunctioned, and that the driver of the big rig was pressing the gas at the instant of impact in an apparent attempt to dodge the crossing gates and beat what he thought was a slow-moving freight train. The information from these black boxes will prove very useful both in insurance claims by the victims as well as in the trial of the truck driver.

So now that we've looked at the black box's features and functions and seen how it's currently used in planes, trains, and automobiles, let's look at some of the new and upcoming developments stemming from this technology. One of the more recent of these developments can be seen according to CNN, December 1, 1999, in the area of the private auto industry. General Motors has unveiled a line of cars in their 2000 inventory which contains an automobile-sized "flight" data recorder.

Whereas *USA Toda,y* June 3, 1999, points out that other manufacturers do have devices which do monitor events at the instant of impact—such as whether the airbag deploys properly—the General Motors version will be the first to actually record data continuously like a flight data recorder does on an aircraft.

This will allow it to monitor conditions, such as seat belt position, brake use, and speed, both before and during the impact. However, the private auto industry has not finished with the black box. According to ABC News, October 29, 1999, research is underway on a device which would not only monitor the car's condition, but which would sense an abrupt change in speed, direction, or orientation (such as if the car slammed into something or flipped) and would then dial dispatchers directly, even telling them what kind of help was needed at the scene—a distinct advantage if the driver happens to be injured or unconscious . . . and if the car happens to be on fire, or trapped underwater.

Interestingly enough, though even this is not the most exciting area of application for data recording technology. That distinction belongs to an entirely different industry. The Emergency Care Research Institute in December of 1999 tells us that a black box has been developed for the human heart. This device, which began as a surgical implant just under the skin of a patient's chest, has now become what is known as the Holter Monitor. Now the Holter Monitor is essentially a tape recorder which is worn on the patient's belt and attached to the patient's chest via electrodes. This allows the patient to monitor their own information and to print that information out directly from the monitor or to upload onto the nearest computer for analysis.

Wonderfully though, even this is not the limit of data recording technology: *USA Today* January 26, 1999, [reports] research is underway on a device which would monitor the human body's every vital function. This device would even allow for live monitoring from a remote location via the Internet, and has already been tested in a Boston Marathon and a coast-to-cost bicycle race and in an ascent of Mt. Everest.

Now that we have looked the black box's features and functions, seeing how it is currently used, and seeing some of the new and exciting areas into which it's technology is expanding, we can see that this device is developed to save lives [and] continues to do just that in ever-increasing circles.

So the next time you're out on the runway waiting for your flight to take off, realize that it could be your flight to become the next unsolved air crash due to previously undiscovered problems—were it not for the efforts of a device known simply as the Black Box.